My Struggles to Freedom

"And ye shall know the truth, and the truth shall make you free."

Robert F. Rhodes

Preface

What I have written about is a series of struggles I encountered over a period of forty-three years in pastoral ministry. They are not unlike the struggles that most of you had to face and overcome during your lifetime. If you are younger, you have not faced many of the struggles yet, but they will come. If you are older, you have faced these struggles and then some. At any rate, we all face struggles that must be overcome to become victorious Christians.

Nothing comes easy in the Christian life. We have an adversary who never lets up in his pursuit of making us miserable. He constructs circumstances in our lives that only with God's help can we overcome. Paul says that to believe in Christ is to suffer for His sake (Philippians 1:29). He also says that godly living brings persecution (2 Timothy 3:12). In spite of it all, however, if we continue in our struggles, the end result is freedom. We can look back and with a sigh of relief say, "It was worth it all."

God sends chastening (corrective punishment) to be endured as proof we are sons of God (Hebrews 12:7). Then He makes us partakers of His holiness, and He causes us to enjoy the peaceable fruit of righteousness (Hebrews 12:10–11). This end result of chastening is freedom and that freedom ensures that we experience the abundant Christian life (John 10:10). The freedom I enjoy is worth the struggles I had to endure.

Table of Contents

Acknowledgements

First, I want to thank my lovely and sweet daughter for all her hard work in putting this book together in a sensible way. It would have been a helter-skelter piece of work if she had not taken the initiative and arranged it so beautifully. Thank you, Sandra. Then, my wonderful niece in creating such a beautiful book cover. I told her it was so nice that it made me want to go out and buy a book right away. Thank you. Sue, for a job well done. I acknowledge and appreciate all the hard work that my granddaughter, Christy Burke, put in on the completion of the book. She composed and edited the blurbs on the cover as well as a myriad of other things. Thank you, Christy, for your hard work. I would be remiss if I did not thank my wonderful wife for the encouragement I received from her when I wanted to quit. There were times when my writing made no sense, but she kept on telling me to press on. I thank you, Marcella, for your confidence in me. And, of course, there is Mike Stroven, who brought his high tech knowledge into the picture and put the finishing touches to the book, Thank you, Mike. If anything good comes from the publishing of this book, it will be because of the splendid team I had working on it. Thank all of you from the bottom of my heart.

Foreword

Summarizing a lifetime of lessons in a few pages of print is no easy task, but Pastor Rhodes has distilled the best of many years of experience into easy to digest chapters called My Struggle to Freedom.

Typical of Pastor Robert F. Rhodes, this book is replete with wisdom, humility, and honesty, and truly manifests grace under pressure. Dr. Rhodes shows the same gracious spirit in his sunset years as he did when I sat under his ministry in the early 1960's. God used his faithful preaching of the Word and the consistent example of his life to awaken in me the realization that God owned me and was calling me to abandon my life to the cause of the Great Commission.

It has been rightly said that a person becomes what he becomes by the influence of the books he reads and the people he meets. My wife, Charlene, and I can attest to the influence of Pastor Rhodes and his wife, Marcella, on our lives as they modeled how Spirit-controlled Christians are supposed to live. We were watching two people live with grace under pressure and did not realize that our lives were being prepared for some unexpected struggles as we were fulfilling the calling of God on our lives.

The transparency of the author will be refreshing and encouraging to anyone who can identify with what it means to face struggles and will also set a pattern for a Godly response when disappointment comes. Those in vocational ministry will especially gain valuable insights from the experiences of Pastor Rhodes which will cause them to realize that they are not the only ones who experience less than ideal circumstances. Someone has said that most people are in a storm, coming out of a storm, or going into a storm. We can all relate to struggles in big things as well as in the common pressures of life.

The lessons I learned from Pastor Rhodes, when God privileged me to be his assistant pastor for many years, were more than I can enumerate. Because of his unselfish nature, I was able to grow in many areas of ministry. His constant encouragement helped me to realize that God could use us if we were willing. He would often quote Zechariah 4:6, ". . . Not by might, nor by power, but by my spirit, saith the Lord of hosts." When human fear would crop up, his counsel was always a reminder that the work of God cannot be done in the arm of the flesh but by the power of the Holy Spirit.

My Struggles to Freedom convicted me, refreshed me, and reminded me of the great unwarranted blessing when God allowed the path of this flawed servant to be intersected by Pastor Robert F. Rhodes: my model, my mentor, my friend.

Les Ollila
January, 2011

Chapter 1

My Struggle with Sin

I knew nothing about salvation until a girl changed my focus from thinking about myself to thinking about God. No, it's not the usual story with her being a Christian and me as that unsaved boy who, through her witness, found the Lord. We were high school sweethearts, both unsaved and doing what unsaved sweethearts do (but no sex). I thought she was beautiful and planned to make her my wife someday. But she could be an agitator, goading me to lose my temper. I was able to tolerate it most of the time, but this one particular night I lost it and got so angry that I slapped her and walked out of the house in a rage. The next thing that happened surprised even me. I looked up to heaven and said, "This time, I'm going with You, God." I don't know what possessed me to say such a thing, except that maybe it was the last straw in a series of events that I now know was God convicting me of my sinful condition.

I was no longer that happy-go-lucky guy just out of high school with no goals, but a sad figure of misery warmed over. I would go to a dance and be the life of the party while there, but, when I got home, I would go into my misery mode. I really did not know what was happening to me, but I knew I needed a change of some sort. Maybe that was why I made that statement. I had tried everything else, so now I would try God.

ᴥ The First Steps to Finding An Answer ᴥ

Many would say it was just an emotional thing that would pass, but God didn't see it that way. He took me seriously. He would give me no peace until I was willing to go to church. My experience with church was not good. I remember during the Second World War, my Sunday school teacher taught that the Japanese would go to heaven even though they believed their emperor was God. She taught us that since their beliefs were sincere, they would go to heaven. I was unsaved, but I knew that was not true. I knew just enough Bible to know that God alone was the way to heaven.

I went to church anyway, not the one with the mixed-up Sunday school teacher, but the one up the street. I had visited it once before when the furnace was not working in our own church, and I went there to get warm. Happily, I visited a Sunday school class where the teacher taught the Bible, so I felt this church would help me with my problem. I really enjoyed the services, even though I felt the pastor had been reading my mail from all the things (I thought) he knew about me. About six weeks passed, and I thought I was ready to join this church, but to join one had to go up front. I was afraid to do that, so I waited until the pastor said, "The angels in heaven are watching you." That was it! I reasoned, if the angels were watching me, they were watching one miserable person who was in need of something better, and I thought it was to join the church. I went forward with the idea that joining the church would solve my problems, but the pastor had other ideas. He looked me squarely in the eyes and asked, "Are you willing to receive Jesus Christ as your

Savior?" I thought just a short moment and reasoned in my mind, "Who wouldn't?" I answered, "Yes."

⨯ I Found The Answer ⨯

From that time on, my life was changed. I had no accompanying bells that rang or whistles that blew, but I knew from that moment on I would surely go to heaven when I died because I had Jesus in my heart. Now I knew what my stepdad's brother meant when he said I had to be saved before I could go to heaven. He had come to spend some time at our house at about the time I was having my problem. I asked him one night how to know you would go to heaven when you died. His answer surprised me. He said you had to be saved before you could go to heaven. Now I knew what he meant.

I later learned that church membership had nothing to do with being saved. It was my belief in Jesus Christ and in Him alone that saved me. He died on the cross to save sinners such as myself. "For Christ also hath once suffered for sins, the just for the unjust, that he might bring us to God, being put to death in the flesh, but quickened by the Spirit" (1 Peter 3:18).

Chapter 2

My Struggle with the Call to Preach

*A*fter settling into salvation, baptism, and church membership, I had an insatiable desire to read and study the Bible, which showed in my casual conversations. This enthusiasm caused my fellow workers to give me the nickname "Preacher." I liked the name, but the thought of seriously considering the ministry was very far from my mind. My hesitancy lay in the fact I could not speak before people. In high school I was elected president of my class and to get in front of my classmates and speak was a frightful ordeal. How in the world could I expect to deliver a message before all those people in church? (Later on, judging from the size of my congregations, I realized I had nothing to worry about.) In the midst of this struggle, a buddy invited me to Florida to spend the summer. I quickly agreed, thinking God would forget about me in Florida. I was like Jonah fleeing to Tarshish. We set out on what I thought would be a lot of fun, but what turned out instead to be a very interesting and life-changing experience for me.

⊰ God sends a "Jonah" Storm ⊱

Our five-dollar-a-day hotel (that was the rate in 1947) on the beach was elegant. We spent each day swimming in the ocean, going to the movies, and eating meals in restaurants. We were enjoying life to the fullest—until my money began to run out. I had to decide whether to go home or get a job.

4

Getting a job meant I could still enjoy the good life, but just a little more sparingly. The job as a busboy at Howard Johnson's restaurant paid just enough to be able to meet expenses and continue my new lifestyle. Little did I know the new busboy hired a week later would be God's arrow to point me in the right direction. He was an unashamed atheist bent on either making converts or embarrassing Christians. I came to believe he was the storm sent to bring this "Jonah" back to his senses.

⇒ THANK GOD FOR THE ATHEIST ⇐

He quickly attached himself like a magnet to me. He incessantly asked the same questions before the waitresses, cooks, and dishwashers in the kitchen, "Bob, do you believe in God? Do you believe in heaven? In hell?" I responded in a quiet, sheepish voice that I did. ("Jonahs" don't yell; they whisper.) He emphatically came back with, "Well, I don't!" This menacing tirade continued for many days. One day while we were sitting on the veranda eating lunch and overlooking the street below with its hustle and bustle of people scurrying about, he asked the same questions. Only this time he became more personal, looked me squarely in the eyes, and said, "If I believed what you say you believe, I would be out on that street corner yelling to the top of my lungs and warning people that such a terrible place as hell really exists." I was stunned. I had no answer. I felt like Jonah must have felt when the storm came. I sat in contemplation and seriously considered his rebuke. I knew he was right. Instead of running away from the call to preach, I should have yielded to the Lord's will. My heart was smitten with conviction. I was being selfish and egotistical. I should have put the negative thoughts out of my mind and made whatever sacrifices were necessary to preach the Word.

With his words still pricking my conscience, I returned to my home in Memphis, Tennessee. I tried arguing with God about why I was not qualified to preach His Word, but He would not let me go. Finally, I yielded my life unreservedly to Him. I held nothing back. If He could use this unprofitable servant, He could have all I had to offer. I could not wait to get beside my bed and yield myself to God in whatever He wanted. I forgot about all the negative things that were hindering me. I heard from God that night, not in an audible voice, but my spirit seemed to sense God saying, "Preach Jesus."

That command became my passion for the next forty-three years spent in active pastoral ministry. Much has been accomplished that would not have been done had it not been for that atheist. In that span of time, more than one hundred young people have answered the call for full-time Christian service. My dad, mother, brother, and sisters have been saved. Many lives have been changed, and many souls have been redeemed. It seems strange to thank God for sending an atheist into my life, but I praise His name for sending him. "O the depth of the riches both of the wisdom and knowledge of

God! how unsearchable are his judgments, and his ways past finding out!" (Romans 11:33). Praise His holy name!

⊰ Finding a Bible School ⊱

After responding to God's call, I needed to find a Bible school in which to be trained. I wrote to three Christian colleges for an application. While I was waiting for their replies, another buddy asked me to go duck hunting. I had never been duck hunting, so I thought it would be a good experience. I decided to go with him. The date was set, and early that morning we headed for a cornfield across the river in Arkansas. No sooner had we arrived and hidden ourselves than we heard a flock of Canadian geese honking above. We patiently waited for them to circle the field. It seemed like a lifetime, but slowly they came in lower and lower. When they finally came close enough for us to have hit them with the butts of our shotguns, both my buddy and I jumped out and aimed, but we froze and neither pulled the trigger. Our positions became exposed to the geese, and they immediately flew away. I had heard of "buck fever," when a hunter freezes at the sight of a buck and cannot pull the trigger, but never have I heard of "goose fever." In our quandary we could only resort to laughter. We left the field and returned home, vowing we would never let what happened be known to our friends.

Upon returning home, I found a letter from Bob Jones University awaiting me. I opened the letter and the words in big, bold type stated, "WE NOT ONLY TEACH YOU HOW TO LOAD THE GOSPEL GUN, BUT WE TEACH YOU HOW TO SHOOT IT." I never heard from the other two schools, but that didn't matter; I knew which school I would attend. I spent four wonderful years there, met my future bride, and later sent both my daughters to attend. I was assured God was in my "goose fever" incident after all.

Chapter 3

My Struggle with Making Mistakes

"My, pastor, you are up early," said a German lady who had attended our church services in the past. I thought that was a strange greeting since I had just the night before made arrangements to be at her home at 7:00 the next morning. She had called and said if I refused to come right away, she was definitely going to divorce her husband. In effect, she was putting the blame on me if she divorced her husband. I had an unusually busy schedule, but I told her I would be there at 7:00 the next morning. She agreed. I thought everything was settled, until I showed up the next morning and asked the woman about her husband. She said he was still in bed because he always slept late. I thought it was strange that he could be that unconcerned since his wife was threatening to divorce him. I asked, "Did you not call me last night and make arrangements to meet today to talk about your relationship with your husband?" She said no, and it dawned on me that I was at the wrong house. There was another German lady in my congregation with whom I had her confused. I offered my apologies and quickly went to the other house. That was a mistake, but that was not the greatest mistake I made.

⇒ More Embarassing Mistakes ⇐

There was another time I made a mistake by serving the wine before the bread in a communion service. It was embarrassing to have to admit before all those people how dumb I could be. I remember getting in late one night after a long, out-of-town trip that allowed me only two or three hours of sleep before I had to be at church and preach the Sunday message. During the preliminaries right before the offering, I was so groggy that I prayed, "Lord, we thank Thee for *this food*." Everyone laughed, and again I was embarrassed. But, in effect, the money in that offering was going to pay my salary with which I would buy food. So I wasn't too far off by praying that prayer. These were mistakes, but they were not the greatest mistake I made in my ministry.

I made a mistake one time by using the wrong word. It was during a time when our state talked of requiring all Christian schools to have licenses before they could operate. In my usual flamboyant manner, I harangued about how I would treat them if they came to our school. I said, "If they come here, I will tell them to take a long [I meant to say *leap*] in the lake." (Instead, I said *leak*.) Talk about embarrassing! I have never lived that down. There was some good that came out of it, though. A visitor met me at the door after the mishap and said, "This is good. I'm coming back; this is better than Johnny Carson." That still, however, wasn't the greatest mistake I made in my ministry.

Next, I made the mistake of underestimating how sharp the twenty-somethings can be. I got carried away in one of my messages about the age a person should be before he could vote. I objected to the notion that if an eighteen-year-old could carry a gun in the military, he was old enough to vote. In my rebuttal of this idea, I made the statement that I don't pay any attention to anyone unless they are at least thirty years of age. After the service, a young man approached me at the door and said that was an excellent message. He went on to say that it was the finest message he had ever heard me preach. But then he burst my bubble by stating, "But what do I know? *I'm only twenty-eight!*" Again, that was a big mistake, but it was not the greatest mistake I made.

⫘ My Greatest Mistake...with Family ⫘

The greatest mistake I made in my ministry was to place my ministry ahead of my family. After two short ministries in Nebraska and Missouri, I accepted the pastorate of Calvary Baptist Church in Roseville, Michigan. It was a larger church than I had served in the past, and I was determined to be successful at any cost. I plunged into the work with total abandonment. The church began to grow, and the more it grew, the harder I worked. I was oblivious to the toll my focus on work was taking on my family until one night I was babysitting my two daughters who were six and three years old at the time. I put them to bed and returned tothe only form of relaxation I knew in those days, the TV.

My older daughter called out from her bedroom for a drink of water, which I promptly got and went back to my "relaxation." Soon after, she called out again and said she had to go the bathroom. I became a little irritated at this point but allowed her to go. Back to the TV I went. Soon after, she came to me and said she wanted to stay up with me because she was not sleepy. I was really irritated by this time and yelled at her and told her to get back into that bed and not to bother me again. Bill Gothard has stated that we get angry when we feel our rights are violated. I felt I had a right to relax, and my daughter was violating those rights. Stunned at my outburst, she turned and ran back to her bed. For a few moments, I felt justified for my action because I needed to be refreshed for my responsibilities the next day. But then a great sense of remorse came over me for what I had done.

She was only six years old and wanted to be with her daddy for a few moments. I had been so blinded by my own selfishness that I could not see that my daughter only wanted a little time with her daddy. I went into her room, smitten with conviction for my lack of understanding, and with tears I grabbed her in my arms and told her how sorry I was and asked for her forgiveness. I began to realize that night how important my family was to me. What a fool I had been in seeking to be a successful pastor more than a successful father. I began paying attention to her from then on, and the reward has been wonderful. This year, for Father's Day, she sent a card and wrote the following: "Happy Father's Day to a dad who always strives to be what God wants. You've been and are a very loving and consistent dad who gave my life a lot of stability. Because of your faithful prayer for me, God worked and is still at work in my life."

I learned the truth of Luke 6:38 that day: "Give and it will be given to you. A good measure, pressed down, shaken together and running over, will be poured into your lap. For with the measure you use, it will be measured to you" (NIV).

Chapter 4

My Struggle with Complaining

*O*ne night, our younger daughter woke up in the middle of the night complaining that she could not breathe. I called our doctor, and he suggested we take her to the shower and allow the steam to open her airways. This was unsuccessful, so I called the local hospital. After assuring them that I had already called our doctor, the hospital allowed me to bring my daughter to the emergency room. Tests revealed a blood sugar count of more than 450. She was on the verge of going into a diabetic coma. Insulin therapy was begun immediately, and I was sent home to wait for the results. Needless to say, the remainder of the night was spent in urgent prayer for the Lord to intervene. For the next six weeks, uncertainty prevailed as to whether our daughter would live or die. My wife and I struggled at the thought of our daughter dying. Visions of her body lying in a casket kept haunting us. I complained to the Lord that this should not be happening, but the more I complained, the worse I felt. The rest of this story will be told at the end of this chapter.

⌛ COMPLAINERS ⚋ SOLUTIONS ⌛

I found that complaining was no solution to any problem. Someone has said that a complainer is an evangelist of grief who is zealous for converts and very difficult to resist. I was not looking for a solution to my problem, but for sympathy. My complaint centered on my dissatisfaction with my circumstances and my disappointment with God. I took little comfort in Moses' complaint that it had not been his idea to lead the people and his request for God to kill him (Numbers 11:10-15). Nor did I find comfort in David's complaint against his enemies and the troubles brought by the wicked (Psalm 55:2–3).

It seems that we are forever complaining about our circumstances. The weather is either too hot or too cold. Our jobs are either too boring or too hard, our wages are too small, our clothes are either too tight or out of style, and on and on it goes. We are never satisfied. Most people complain because of frustrated expectations. A job promotion never came through or the expected raise never happened. Married couples complain because their spouses are not meeting their needs. We never expected our little girl to have diabetes.

Habakkuk's expectations were also too high. He was God's prophet and expected things to happen when he cried out to God. There were sinful conditions in Judah, but God turned a deaf ear (Habakkuk 1:2–4). Habakkuk's credibility was at stake; he felt God had let him down. Habakkuk felt that he had become like thunder and lightning without rain. He was in danger of becoming a laughingstock. He desperately sought answers to his dilemma. He found it incredible that God would not answer him. But God had a reason for stonewalling Habakkuk; He had another plan, a plan that was unbelievable. "I will work a work in your days, which ye will not believe, though it be told you" (Habakkuk 1:5). God had a plan to use the godless Chaldeans to punish Judah (Habakkuk 1:6). His plan was to do the unthinkable to the unsuspecting with unexpected results. God reserves the freedom to initiate and work His own plan.

✂ HABAKKUK - NOT HAPPY WITH GOD'S PLAN ✂

But Habakkuk was not happy with God's plan, and he complained about it. He could not accept that God would use a people to punish Judah who actually needed punishment themselves. He tried to reason with God that surely He was so pure and holy that He could not do such a thing (Habakkuk 1:12–13). He saw only the circumstances surrounding him, which blinded his spiritual perception of God. But God had planned to judge the Chaldeans by causing their own victims, their own unjust ways, their own violence, and their own idolatry to bring them down (Habakkuk 2:6–20). God was putting into effect the universal law of reaping and sowing even then (Galatians 6:7).

✂ COMPLAINING MUST BE DIRECTED TO GOD ✂

I began to ask myself if complaining was ever justified, and I found, through Habakkuk, that it was, but certain criteria must be met. First, it is right to complain when the complaint is directed to God. Jeremiah made a serious complaint that he was made a laughingstock and everyone mocked him because of the Word of the Lord, but Jeremiah made his complaint to the Lord and was exonerated (Jeremiah 20:7–8). The psalmist was careful to direct his complaint only to the Lord (Psalm 142:2). Job complained only to the Lord (Job 21:4), and Habakkuk made his complaint to the Lord (Habakkuk 1:2). I was encouraged because I, too, had directed my complaint to the Lord. I can find no record in the Bible of any spiritual person ever directing his complaint to anyone but God.

⫷ COMPLAINTS? FROM A GRIEVING HEART ⫸

Second, the complaint must come from a grieving heart. I certainly met this criteria; my heart was breaking for my little girl who was lying in the hospital. I did not know whether she would live or die. Jeremiah had a grieving heart when he complained, "Cursed be the day wherein I was born" (Jeremiah 20:14). Hannah grieved in her complaint for not being able to have a child (1 Samuel 1:10). Job also made his complaint out of grief: "Therefore I will not refrain my mouth; I will speak in the anguish of my spirit; I will complain in the bitterness of my soul" (Job 7:11). Grief-motivated complaints are welcomed by the Lord; all others are shunned.

⫷ WILLING TO ABIDE BY GOD'S ANSWER ⫸

I learned the third reason for a justifiable complaint from Habakkuk also. We must be willing to abide by the answer God gives. Habakkuk realized that God's greater purpose was better than his finite plan, and he readily accepted it and became content with whatever God ordered. He was content knowing that God was going to judge the Chaldeans also (Habakkuk 2:8). He finally learned to rejoice in God whatever his circumstances (Habakkuk 3:17–19). I learned, too, that freedom from complaining comes when I understand

God's purposes supersede my own selfish circumstances and I step aside to allow Him to work His plan.

❯❮ THE REST OF THE STORY ❯❮

Now, for the rest of the story. Because of my misery and desperation, I finally yielded to whatever fate God had for my daughter (even her death), and I agreed to accept His will above all. The peace I felt was immediate. My joy returned. Everything was all right again with me and the Lord. All because I found my place in submission and not in complaining. Forty-five years later, my daughter is a university graduate, a mother and grandmother, and the wife of my pastor. God is good.

Chapter 5

My Struggle with What Is Fair or Right

$\mathcal{S}$everal years ago in Michigan, an eleven-year-old girl was repeatedly raped over a period of time by her mother's boyfriend. She became pregnant and wanted an abortion, but her mother refused. The state went to court to overturn the mother's wishes, but the judge ruled against it. There was an outcry claiming unfairness for his ruling. Strong sentiment arose on both sides. Some felt it unfair to make this innocent little girl carry this selfish brute's baby. Others believed strongly that the killing of an innocent baby was terribly wrong. But the judge ruled on what he felt was right instead of what some thought was fair.

I'll have to admit, I had a struggle with the judge's decision. Because of my empathy for the girl, I thought this might be a justifiable reason for the abortion. I mistakenly allowed my emotions to settle on what was fair and not on what was right. To settle my quandary, I searched the Scriptures. I found that God had also made some decisions that some would call unfair. He ordered the destruction of the earth by water, which included small children (Genesis 6:12–13, 17). Many would call this brutal and terribly unfair. He ordered the destruction of Sodom and Gomorrah, which also included small children (Genesis 18: 20–21; 19:24–25). Some would say it was terribly unfair for Him to order Abraham to kill his son (Genesis 22:2–18). In each of these instances, however, God operated from a sense of justice and not from fairness. Abraham said, "Shall not the Judge of all the earth do right?" (Genesis 18:25). God can only do right, whether it appears fair or not. I began to see that the judge had the best interests of the girl in mind, whether it appeared fair or not. He knew that abortions affect future pregnancies; women who have abortions experience higher miscarriage and mortality rates, so the judge ruled against the abortion.

⧐⧏ JUSTICE VS. FAIRNESS ⧐⧏

Too often, we allow our sentiments to hinder the workings of God, who always has our best interests at heart. God has always been right in all His judgments: the flood, the destruction of Sodom and Gomorrah, the killing of the firstborn in Egypt. Man's sinful condition renders him incapable of judging what is right, so he judges what is fair, and what is right does not appear fair to him. So man holds God accountable for his own sense of fairness and blames God when He acts differently.

A perfect example of the difference between right and fair is when Peter asked a question about rewards in Matthew 19:27: "Behold, we have forsaken all, and followed thee; what shall we have therefore?" Jesus answered with an illustration of a landowner who needed workers. He made a contract with the first batch for a denarius (Matthew 20:2). The landowner needed more workers and went back to the market place to obtain more. This time the landowner agreed to pay what was right (no contract, just a promise) (Matthew 20:3–4). He went back three more times to hire additional help with the same promise he made to the second group (Matthew 20:5–7). At the end of the day, he paid them all the same (Matthew 20:9).

The first group complained that they should have received more because they worked longer (Matthew 20:11–12). They didn't think the landowner was being fair. To this he answered that he paid them what he agreed to pay and that he had done no wrong (Matthew 20:13–14). In other words, he was right even though it seemed he was being unfair. This answered Peter's question about rewards. Rewards will be awarded to the faithful by what God deems right and not according to man's expectations. "So the last will be first, and the first will be last" (Matthew 20:16 NIV).

⸎ GOD IS ALWAYS RIGHT AND FAIR ⸎

God is always right and fair because He is God. Men and women of God have never been concerned with what is fair, but what is right. What was fair about Abraham being promised a son for an heir and then being ordered to murder him (Genesis 22:2)? Abraham never complained when Lot was given the plains with the best water supply for his cattle (Genesis 13:8–12). He was not concerned with fairness, but with right. Abraham had an implicit faith that if God ordered it, it was right, no matter how unfair it might seem. He never questioned that God had a purpose in whatever He chose to do (Romans 8:28–29).

Was it fair for Moses—who had wealth, fame, and a prosperous future—to forfeit it all because he wanted to obey God and do right? Was it fair for him to flee Egypt as a common criminal for defending one of his countrymen (Exodus 2:11–15)? Was it fair for the people to blame him when

20

Pharaoh placed extra burdens on them (Exodus 5:18–21)? Moses was not concerned with fairness, but with what was right. Was it fair for Job to lose his fortune, his children, and his health for "no reason"? When his friends reprimanded him for getting what he deserved (Job 4:7–8) and the Lord rebuked him for even trying to find the purpose for his misfortunes (Job 38:16–20), was that fair? Job was not even remotely concerned with the unfairness of what was happening to him, because he knew that whatever took place, his trust was in the Lord (Job 13:15).

Joseph never yelled, "Unfair," about being betrayed by his brothers (Genesis 37:27–28) or about the lies of Potiphar's wife and the subsequent imprisonment (Genesis 39:17–20). He saw beyond the initial disappointments to the ultimate purpose of God. "Ye thought evil against me; but God meant it unto good, to bring to pass, as it is this day, to save much people alive" (Genesis 50:20).

What is fair about not resisting evil or turning the other cheek (Matthew 5:39), about loving your enemies (Matthew 5:44) or suffering for something you did not do (1 Peter 2:18–21)? There was nothing fair about the trial and execution of Jesus, but it had to be right because God ordered it for the salvation of the world. Godly men never questioned the fairness of their circumstances; their only concern was to do right and to respond positively, acknowledging that "the Judge of the earth [will] do right" (Genesis 18:25).

Chapter 6

My Struggle with Marriage

*A*s of this writing, my wife and I have been married for fifty-eight years. They have been the happiest years of my life. We have had our ups and downs, but we never had a disagreement that couldn't be resolved. For example, I was in my fifties, and I felt it was time I had some life insurance. She felt we should trust the Lord to take care of us. I, too, felt we should trust the Lord, but I felt we should trust Him through life insurance. I had a man from an insurance company drop by my office one day, and I bought a life insurance policy. She didn't object when I told her and that insurance policy blossomed into a retirement plan that has financed our retirement for the past thirteen years and continues to do so.

I haven't always been right, though. We had an agreement that we would not make any large purchases without consulting each other. One day, a church member who worked at General Motors called me to come look at a car that was a real bargain. He was not a salesman, but a man who re-worked little flaws in new cars. I looked at the car, agreed it was a bargain, and purchased it without consulting my wife. That was a mistake. That car was a real lemon. I replaced the engine and gave it to my daughter, thinking it would be all right. She ended up replacing the engine in it twice. So much for Mr. Perfection.

✺ A Difference in Personalities ✺

I suppose it is true that opposites attract. My wife and I are complete opposites. I am a choleric, and she is a sanguine. A choleric is a type A personality. Get out of the way when he's coming through. Very impetuous and impatient, he wants things done yesterday. He doesn't have time for people; he's more into projects. A sanguine, on the other hand, is a people person. She never gets upset, is always the people pleaser. Social relationships mean everything to her. She is affected by other people's problems. When a person loses a spouse, she prays for the survivor for months.

Some people look upon these differences as a bad thing. Because they do not understand each other, they give up. My wife and I have an understanding that "we will NEVER understand each other." Where in the Bible does it say that a husband and wife are to understand each other? It says they are to love one another (Ephesians 5:25, Titus 2:4). If you love each other, you will accept each other, whether you understand or not. Love has no expectations. It accepts others as they are. It is these differences, however, that allow us the opportunity to submit ourselves one to another in the fear of God (Ephesians 5:21). My wife has certain strengths that I don't have. I am to submit to those strengths. Her strength is social relationships; I am to submit to that strength. My strength is organization; she is to submit to that strength.

✺ Focus, Responsibility & Position ✺

My wife and I started out focusing on each other's weaknesses. We didn't want to focus on each other's strengths

23

because doing that only highlighted our own weaknesses. When we focused on our strengths, we could not see our weaknesses. This pattern changed when I said to her one day that I had learned a great deal from her. She was shocked into asking the question, "What have I learned from him?" From then on, she began looking at my strengths as an opportunity to overcome her weaknesses. Now, our pattern is to focus on the other's strengths in order to help us overcome our weaknesses. By establishing this pattern, we were able to revolutionize our marriage. In this way we learn from each other.

Concerning the principles of home management, the wife should submit to the husband because he is her head. In order for the husband to establish the right principles in the home, however, he must submit to his Head, the Lord Jesus (1 Corinthians 11:3). Those things in which each submits to the other concern individual behavior. For example, he is to submit to her in matters that concern people and their needs, and she is to submit to him in matters that deal with things and ideas (car and home repairs, vocational advice for the children). These principles will work regardless of the personality profiles of each. Adjustments will need to be made whether she is a choleric and he is a sanguine.

God never says that man is superior to the woman. The husband does, however, have a God-given position as head of the wife (Ephesians 5:23) as Christ is the head of the church. But does that mean he is superior to her? By no means. He also has a Head, and he is to set the example of submission as he submits to his Head (1 Corinthians 11:3). As head of the wife, the husband holds the responsibility to stay in right relationship with his Head to better understand his wife's position. In addition, he has been given that authority for the purpose of edification (2 Corinthians 10:8). In other words, the husband has been given his authority to build up the family, not tear it down. This authority is not to boost his image as if he were some know-it-all who never makes a mistake, who is right with every decision he makes. He should remember he is human and prone to the same mistakes as anyone else.

❯❮ THE ANSWER? LOVE... ❯❮

It is interesting that God said that the husband is to love his wife as he loves himself (Ephesians 5:28). He goes on to say that "no man ever yet hated his own flesh" (Ephesians 5:29). He knows us pretty well. Man is so egotistical that he has chapped lips from kissing himself in the mirror. It is because of this ego that it is so difficult for him to express his love for his wife. I heard of a man who—when asked by his wife why he didn't tell her he loved her—replied, "Listen, I told you twenty years ago I loved you, and if I ever changed my mind, I'd let you know." Wives cannot take for granted that their husbands love them. They need to hear love spoken daily from their husbands.

I had a difficult time adjusting to marriage. I grew up as an only child who never had to share anything with anybody. I never had to consider another person because our family consisted of just my mother and me, and she worked during the day. Consequently, I did my own thing and enjoyed every minute of it. When I got married, all that came to a screeching halt. I remember one time I promised my wife I would pick her up after baseball practice. I got so involved in the practice that I forgot all about her. I was late picking her up, but I thought that was no big deal because she would understand. Boy, was I wrong! She got in the car and didn't say a word, but I noticed she screwed up her face and a tear rolled down her cheek. Pretty soon, there was a deluge of tears. I certainly didn't expect that. Why couldn't she bawl me out? That would have felt much better than having to see all those tears.

The husband is to love his wife as Christ loves the church (Ephesians 5:25). How does Christ love the church? He accepts us the way we are. He takes us with all our warts and loves us anyway. When we ultimately decide we need to change, He sets the proper example for us to go by. He understands our frustrations and listens (without comment) empathetically. He never criticizes us, no matter our faults, but praises us instead. He constantly reaffirms His love for us. Husbands, do you love your wives this way? You can pretend you love your wife and put on a pious look as if you do, but until you love her as Christ loved the church, you are just pretending.

Chapter 7

My Struggle with Expectations

*A*n epitaph read, "I expected this, but not just yet!" Another said, "I told you that I was sick!" Though we may laugh at these, the time each individual will face death is truly uncertain. In fact, almost everything in life is uncertain. Someone has said, "The only certainty is uncertainty." The unexpected happens regardless of our best efforts to remain certain. While I was preparing for the ministry, I expected, once I was in the ministry, that I would receive love and respect because of my position. Was I in for a shock. I was called to a certain church, and they were discussing where I would live. One of the elders made the statement, "I don't care if he lives in a piano box." So much for love and respect. I never expected church members at a business meeting to rail about my ineffectiveness then walk out never to return, but it happened.

I never expected my nine-year-old daughter to nearly die from diabetes, but it happened. I thought God would spare my family from such debilitating illnesses, but He chose instead to be with us in our affliction. Job never expected all ten of his children to be killed, even though he prayed for them. I was more fortunate than Job. My daughter was spared and except for losing sight in her right eye, she is a normal fifty-four-year-old adult female. New believers have a difficult time with expectations. They expect to have instant spiritual maturity, which comes only with testing and adversity. They expect to have advanced Bible knowledge without putting in years of hard work and study. They look for the easy way instead of the right way.

⋺⋲ SPOUSAL EXPECTATIONS ⋺⋲

Husbands and wives have a particularly difficult time with expectations. He is the perfect gentleman before marriage, and she is the ideal mate. In the courting stage, each meets the criteria of the "ideal" they concocted years before. This concept of the "ideal" carries over into marriage, until each falls short of that concept. They then begin to compare their actual mates with their "ideal" mates. But this is unfair because their "ideal" mates have no faults. She is confident her "ideal" would never come home late, throw his clothes on the floor, yell at the least bit of irritation, or be unable to admit he was wrong. Her faults become clear when he begins to compare his "ideal" with her incessant talking on the phone, spending too much time with the kids, running up charges on the credit card, or not being submissive to him. These comparisons will continue until each realizes the "ideal" mate does not exist. Their actual mate is the "ideal." It is up to the other to make each the "ideal." They do this by showing the other by example what they expect of an ideal mate. If she expects him to be more gentle and kind, she is to be an object lesson of gentleness and kindness in her behavior. If he expects her to be more submissive, he is to exemplify submissiveness to those in authority over him.

At a men's Bible class years ago, I asked what men expected of their wives. The first thing listed was perpetual beauty. A man's first interest is the looks of a woman. I reminded them of the verse that says to "rejoice with the wife of thy youth" (Proverbs 5:18). It does not say, "rejoice with the youth of thy wife." Among other things, the men wanted a "buddy" relationship, and, of course, a submissive spirit. Their list consisted of thirteen expectations. I asked what they could do to help their wives meet those expectations, but got no response.

I later asked a ladies' group their expectations of their husbands. They desired a spiritual leader, first and foremost, who would conduct family devotions and be faithful at church. They wanted a man who would have intimate communication with them, never raise his voice, and admit when he was wrong. They felt he should spend time with their children, discipline them with kindness, and train them in spiritual values.

⊰ THE "LAWS" OF EXPECTATIONS ⊱

These expectations have a way of becoming "laws" or standards of behavior by which each punishes the other when expectations are not met. He punishes her by working late, staying out with friends, or griping and complaining about the least little thing. I heard of a man who said, "I'm going home and if supper isn't ready, I'll complain, and if it is, I won't eat it." There is no pleasing a man like that. He feels justified in not helping with housework or taking her out because of "laws" she has broken, whether she has or not. Most

29

of the time a wife has no idea when and if she broke any of the husband's laws because he won't tell her.

She punishes by nagging or losing interest in doing housework, being involved with his interests, or being physically intimate. She may find herself agreeing with Marie Coreli, an English novelist of the nineteenth century, "who was a spinster and liked it. When asked by her friends why she never married, she inevitably replied: 'There is no need. I have three pets at home which serve the same purpose as a husband. I have a dog that growls all morning, a parrot that swears all afternoon, and a cat that comes home late at night.'"1 To compensate for the lack of attention from her husband, a wife will often spend an inordinate amount of time with her girlfriends or take an outside job or become obsessed with the children.

⊰ THE SOLUTION? BIBLICAL LOVE ⊱

The solution for both husband and wife is twofold—throw away all expectations and practice biblical love. Biblical love does not keep a running account of things done against it (1 Corinthians 13:5 NIV). If a wife practices biblical love (which is long-suffering), she is not disappointed if he comes home late. If he expects a clean house when he comes home, by practicing biblical love he will not be disappointed if it is not cleaned up because biblical love is not easily angered (1 Corinthians 13:5 NIV). In fact, if he is motivated to clean the house himself, she will respond to his kindness and will gladly submit to him. She is responsive by nature and will respond in like fashion to any act of kindness shown to her. Obviously, he is not expected to do this every day. She probably had unforeseen emergencies that day. The point is that the more you give, the more you will receive.

My wife and I have worked at marriage for more than fifty years and it has worked, although we had a little difficulty the first year of our marriage. We lived in an apartment that had a gas stove, and she had always had electric stoves in her home. One day, she intended to light the gas burner but forgot the match. She left the gas switch open and went to get a match. When she returned with the match and struck it, the accumulated gas blew up. Happily, she was not hurt, not even a singed hair. My response was to rant and rave about why you should never turn on the gas before you strike a match. But she didn't need a safety lecture; she needed sympathy. She had just been through a very traumatic experience, and the last thing she needed was a lecture. I eventually learned to be tender and understanding in such experiences.

My wife and I have an understanding that we will never understand each other. We may love each other, but we will never understand each other. Our interests are not the same. When men get together, they talk about cars, sports, and work. Women talk about children, people, and surgeries they have had. Men take things for granted, women do not. That is why wives must be told that husbands love them every day. They don't take anything for granted. But men do. When men are working on a project together, they don't waste time with words; they just grunt when they want something.

Women, on the other hand, talk to express themselves because they take nothing for granted.

✳ BEING IS BETTER THAN DOING ✳

By giving up our expectations, we actually release each other from the pressure of trying to live up to what others think of us instead of what God knows us to be. God doesn't have expectations for us, because He "knoweth our frame; he remembereth that we are dust" (Psalm 103:14). All He expects of us is that we be faithful and obey His Word. Some have made the mistake of doing things to please the Lord without realizing He is more interested in who we are than in what we do. Micah tells us simply what the Lord requires of us: "He hath shewed thee, O man, what is good; and what doth the LORD require of thee, but to do justly, and to love mercy, and to walk humbly with thy God?" (Micah 6:8). God desires that we work on *being* rather than *doing*. Fulfilling others' expectations is doing; having no expectations and simply obeying God is being.

Chapter 8

My Struggle with Forgiveness

$\mathcal{M}$y ten-year-old daughter was asked to babysit a neighbor's two young children. I hesitated at first because she had recently been diagnosed with diabetes and had passed out twice since she had returned home from the hospital a few weeks earlier. But since the family lived just across the street from our home, we allowed her to go. Unfortunately, she had an attack and passed out while there. Fortunately, the neighbor was still home and called us immediately. We rushed over with the remedy, and in a few minutes she was normal.

The incident was no big deal to my wife and me, but the father had a problem with it and consequently decided not to use my daughter in the future because he felt it would be jeopardizing the safety of his children. I took offense thinking, "How could this guy be so insensitive to my daughter's serious health situation?" Was he so self-centered that he could not be a little empathetic toward my daughter?

I didn't want it to happen, but resentment began to build in my heart. I knew it was wrong because resentment could blossom into full-blown hatred, and I didn't want that. I began to reason that he was just a father protecting his children, and I would do the same. I dealt with the resentment by remembering I should forgive others because I had been forgiven. I never mentioned my resentment to him because he did not cause the problem. I caused it and knew it was up to me to forgive him and regain my peace with the Lord.

33

⊰ FORGIVE TO BE FORGIVEN ⊱

I was again reminded of a basic scriptural principle that to be forgiven by God we must be willing to forgive others first. In the model prayer, Jesus made clear that we are to forgive others or God will not forgive us (Matthew 6:14–15). This theme runs throughout the New Testament (Matthew 18:35; Mark 11:25–26; Luke 6:37, 11:4, 17:3–4; Ephesians 4:32; Colossians 3:13). The Bible makes it abundantly clear that to be forgiven of one's own transgressions against God, one must first be willing to forgive others of their transgressions against him.

Peter asked Jesus how many times he should forgive a brother who had sinned against him—seven times (Matthew 18:21)? Jesus' answer of "seventy times seven" (v. 22) was a hyperbole indicating that Peter should not be concerned about the number of times to forgive a brother who sins, but the development of a spirit of forgiveness that keeps on forgiving, regardless of the number of times the brother sins. Let's say that you are a worker going about your work with a stack of papers in one hand and a cup of coffee in the other. Another worker comes around a corner too fast and runs into you, causing you to drop those papers, and, worse, the coffee spills all over them and ruins them. He apologizes fervently and helps you clean up the mess. You reluctantly forgive him, but you don't say, "That's one! Just 489 more to go." No, you don't keep a count of times you have been offended. Jesus is teaching that no matter how many times you are offended, you forgive out of a spirit of forgiveness.

To prove His point, Jesus continued with an illustration of a king who had entrusted the affairs of his estate to a trusted servant. When he called the servant into account, the king found him to be in arrears ten thousand talents (about ten million dollars) (v.23–24). The servant could not repay the debt, but a compassionate master forgave him all he owed (vv. 25–27). But that same servant, who had just been forgiven an astronomical amount of money, went to another servant, who owed him a pittance (about eighteen dollars) and demanded he pay up (v. 28). Although the delinquent servant begged for the same mercy the other servant had just received, he was denied it and thrown into prison by the unforgiving servant (vv. 29–30). The king, upon hearing of this refusal to forgive the servant, ordered him to be tortured and required payment of his debt of ten million dollars (vv. 32–35). Jesus closed the illustration by making the point that the Father will not forgive your offense until you forgive your brother his offense (v. 35).

We are told to rebuke a brother who sins, and, if he repents, we are to forgive him (Luke 17:3). You are in another city on a business trip. You happen to see a member of your church in the hotel lounge drinking an alcoholic beverage. What should you do? You could gossip about the incident to another church member and get all pious. Or you could call the pastor and tattletale on him to "get that sin out of our church." According to Luke 17:3, however, you are to rebuke in such a way as to bring about repentance. What he needs is a rebuke and not to be tattled on.

So you walk into the lounge and sit down with him. He is rebuked just by your presence, even if you do not say a word. He will immediately begin to offer his reasons for being there. It may be he just lost his job or his wife is terminally ill or his children are on drugs. Whatever the reason, he offers his justification. You suggest another place to talk and begin to minister to this unfortunate one, who will probably see the error of his ways and repent. The verse says the rebuke will more than likely bring repentance. In the Greek, "if he repent" means a more probable future condition. Because of the rebuke, a more probable future condition is that he would repent. So don't hesitate to rebuke a brother if you see him sinning, but do it in such a way as to bring about repentance.

✂ FORGIVENESS IS NOT BY FAITH? ✂

The disciples thought that developing this spirit of forgiveness was by faith, but Jesus taught otherwise (Luke 17:4–5). Faith is commendable and can uproot trees (Luke 17:6), but faith is not required to establish a forgiving spirit. Jesus illustrated this point by saying that a slave is not told by his master to sit down at a meal after a hard day's work in the field. No, it is the slave's responsibility to get the meal for his master before he eats his own food. He receives no thanks for his actions because he is only doing what he has been commanded to do. We are to develop a forgiving spirit because it is our duty as obedient servants (Luke 17:7–10).

Someone has said that a trespass is not forgiven until one forgets it. But the Bible never says to forget a trespass. Sometimes it is impossible to forget a serious wrong. God does not forget our trespasses because He is omniscient (all-knowing). But He can will not to remember them. "For I will forgive their wickedness and will remember their sins no more" (Jeremiah 31:34). We may not forget a trespass, but we can *will* not to remember it.

A young Greenlander said to a missionary: "I do love Jesus—I would do anything for him; how good of him to die for me!" Said the missionary: "Are you *sure* you would do anything for our dear Lord?" "Yes, I would. What can I do?" The missionary showing him the Bible said, "This book says, 'Thou shalt do no murder.'" "Oh, but that man killed my father." "Our dear Lord himself says, 'If ye love me, keep my commandments,' and this is one of them." "Oh," exclaimed the Greenlander, "I do love Jesus! But I—must . . ." "Wait a little, calm yourself, think it well over, and then come and let me know." He went out, but presently came back, saying, "I cannot decide; one moment I will, the next I will not. Help me to decide." The missionary answered, "When you say, 'I will kill him,' it is the evil spirit trying to gain the victory; when you say, 'I will not,' it is the Spirit of God striving within you." And so speaking, he induced him at length to give up his murderous design.

Accordingly the Greenlander sent a message to the murderer of his father, telling him to come and meet him as a friend. He came, with kindness on his lips, but treachery in his heart. For, after he had stayed with him a while, he asked the young man to come and visit him on this side of the river. To this he readily assented, but, on returning to his boat, found that a hole had been pierced in the boat, which to the surprise and warmth and indignation of the other, who had climbed a high rock on purpose to see him drown, did not sink, but merrily breasted the waves. Then cried the young man to his enemy, "I freely forgive you, for our dear Lord has forgiven me."[2]

Chapter 9

My Struggle with Depression

I thought depression would never happen to me. I looked at depression as a lack of trust in God or as self-pity. I thought I had good, sound reasonable evidence that depression was a matter of the will because Proverbs 25:28 says, "He that hath no rule over his own spirit is like a city that is broken down, and without walls." That verse tells us that it is possible for anyone to rule his own spirit and that it was the person's own fault if he or she were depressed. Jay Adams said, "Depression is not inevitable, something that simply happens and cannot be avoided. Nor is it ever so far gone that the depression cannot be counteracted. The cycle can always be reversed at any point by biblical action in the power of the Holy Spirit. The hope for depressed persons, as elsewhere, lies in this: the depression is the result of the sin. If depression were some strange, unaccountable malady that has overcome him, for which he is not responsible and consequently about which he can do nothing, hope would evaporate."[3]

⊰ MY EXPERIENCE WITH DEPRESSION ⊱

But that was before my experience with depression. My wife and I were visiting her sister and husband in Florida. One night I woke up and felt very dizzy and on the way to the bathroom I held on to the walls to keep from falling. In the bathroom I fell on my hands and knees and could not get up. It took a trip to the emergency room and three days of rest to bring me out of my stupor. Two months later, I had a more severe case of the same thing. Only this time it did not go away. I have had consultations with four specialists, and they all agree that a virus caused my problem. I am being treated with medication.

Shortly after my second bout, a tremendous depression set in. I have never experienced such a terrible assault on my physical, emotional, and spiritual powers. It seemed as if I had no power to resist, that some strange power had overtaken me and I was helpless to resist. I cried out to the Lord, and it seemed as if He had forsaken me. I was unable to get help from anywhere or from anyone. As a result, I found myself not caring about whether I lived or died. In fact, I had thoughts about how wonderful it would be if I could die and end all the misery. I felt trapped within my body and wanted desperately to get out. I had no desire to be with my wife of more than fifty years nor did I care to associate with any of my friends.

⊃⊂ EFFECTS OF DEPRESSION ⊃⊂

I found in Psalm 55 what I thought described my situation rather accurately. The psalmist begged for God's attention and for God not to hide from his supplication (v. 1); he was restless in his complaint and was distracted (v. 2). In the same way, I felt abandoned in a deep, dark hole by God and everyone. My sleep left me. I lay awake for hours fighting the fear of rejection and discouragement. The psalmist was bothered by the slanderous tirades of his enemies and the pressures of their anger (v. 3). My enemies were my thoughts. I heard voices flailing away at my character and predicting a terrible doom that would soon ensue. Though I knew it was imagined, it was very real to me and I could not escape it. The uncertainty of life was ever present. Like David, my heart was in anguish and the terrors of death fell upon me and horror overwhelmed me (vv. 4–5). I wished with him that I could fly away and find my refuge away from the stormy circumstances (vv. 6–8). But I was trapped! I could not escape my chains of depression.

꘍ CAUSE OF DEPRESSION REVISITED ꘍

In desperation I went back to my original supposition and examined my life for sin. My good friend Dr. Jim Binney said that depression comes from either a biological problem or a sin problem. My biological problem was very real, but I thought it was more than that. I wondered if I had a sin problem. My pride had kept me from considering this cause. However, in desperation, I was made to see I had been dabbling in the "sin which doth so easily beset us" (Hebrews 12:1). I had been dismissing it as of little consequence since it was my private thought life and no one else could be affected by it. But God made it clear that this sin was the main cause of my depression. I had allowed myself to become a victim of lustful thinking. God used my biological problem to call attention to my greater sin problem.

Jay Adams continued in *The Christian Counselor's Manual*: "The fact is, however, though he may not be responsible for the initial problem (e.g., physical illness or a bad turn in his financial picture), he is responsible for *handling this initial problem God's way.* Because he hasn't, he instead has sinfully reacted to the problem (e.g., neglecting duties and chores;

becoming resentful; complaining in self-pity), subsequently, *as a result of this reaction* he has become depressed."[4] Rather than handling the initial problem God's way, I kept analyzing and investigating what was happening to me (self-pity) instead of looking at the problem as God's way of getting my attention for the real problem in my life—my sin!

✗ Personal: Cause of MY Depression ✗

When it finally dawned on me what was really happening, I immediately fell on my face before God and confessed my sin, admitted my guilt, and begged for Him to take me back into His good graces. My return to normalcy in my spiritual life was almost immediate. The uncertainty was gone. God became near and our fellowship was again sweet. The frightful thoughts disappeared, and I began to live again. I once again enjoyed my dear wife and my friends. It was a wonderful turnaround, and I am enjoying life more than ever. But the physical problem still exists. My vertigo is still with me, but I now look upon it not as a liability, but as a reminder to keep my eyes constantly on the Lord or dire consequences might occur.

Chapter 10

My Struggle with Being Made in God's Image

*W*hen the Bible said we were made in the image of God, it meant we were made like Him socially, morally, and mentally. Paul indicated that we are social creatures by stating, "For none of us liveth to himself, and no man dieth to himself" (Romans 14:7). It is not normal for someone to live to himself. Society calls anyone who does so a hermit or a recluse. God's order of putting us here by families indicates His desire for us to act socially. I was an only child, and my dad left my mother and me for another woman. I still loved him because he was my dad. The emotional tie to a parent is the strongest emotion in spite of the circumstances. God put it into the makeup of humankind to be socially attached to our loved ones. When we hurt, they hurt with us. When we are glad, they are glad with us. There is no stronger bond anywhere than the family bond. God patterned our family after His heavenly family.

In the parable of the prodigal son, Jesus gave us a glimpse of what the heavenly family is like. The father patiently waited for his wayward son to come home. It is the same with some of us. God is patient and waits, sometimes for years, for some of us to come home. "In one of Dr. J. Wilbur Chapman's meetings a man arose to give the following remarkable testimony: 'I got off at the Pennsylvania depot as a tramp, and for a year I begged on the streets for a living. One day I touched a man on the shoulder and said, "Mister, please give me a dime." As soon as I saw his face, I recognized my father. "Father, don't you know me?" I asked. Throwing his arms around me, he cried, "I have found you; all I have is yours." Men, think of it, that I, a tramp, stood begging my father for ten cents, when for eighteen years he had been looking for me to give me all he was worth!'"[5] So the heavenly Father is waiting for us.

It is a wonderful honor to bear the image of God. He never entrusted it to the angels or to the rest of His creation—the animals. He gave it exclusively to the crown of His creation—man. As sincere as the animal rights people are, they do not understand the concept that the image of God is the difference between man and animals. Animals have no souls that can relate to God. Only man has that privilege. Animals are not moral creatures. Neither are they intelligent enough to speak, and, although they have a semblance of a social life, it is based more on instinct than on choice.

Man is to bear the image of God, regardless of his vocation. Whether he is a musician, preacher, school teacher, missionary, secretary, clerk, politician, lawyer, engineer, computer operator, plumber, or doctor, he is to bear the image of God. God never intended there be any criminals, atheists, swindlers, humanists, murderers, or Friedrich Nietzsches. I remember reading several years ago an interesting story about Nietzsche. He had stated that God was dead. A student where Nietzsche taught in the university put a post on the bulletin board that stated: "God is Dead. Signed, Friedrich Nietzsche," and all the other students got a good laugh out of it. Sometime later, Nietzsche also died and a Christian student posted another post that stated: "Nietzsche is Dead. Signed, God." No one laughed.

❧ God's Image Lost ❧

But, sadly, man lost that image when he sinned in the Garden of Eden. He lost it through the subtlety of Satan. The first thing that Satan did was to discredit God. He portrayed God as impersonal, as one who did not have man's best interests at heart. He did it by using the impersonal name for God eight times (Genesis 3:1; 2:4; 7–9; 15–16). Second, he planted doubts in Eve's mind (Genesis 3:1). Satan taunted Eve: "You don't mean to tell me that God actually said you are not to eat of every tree of the garden, do you?" He was setting her up for yet the third attack, lying. He said that God had ulterior motives for giving the command. "He knows when you eat of the forbidden fruit, your eyes will be opened, and you will be his equal" (v. 5). It was a blatant lie. God said, "Thou shall surely die" (2:17) and man has died ever since.

Satan's attack was effective in large part because of Eve's weakness for being deceived. Paul told Timothy that Eve was deceived (1 Timothy 2:14). She actually believed the devil's lie that she would become like God if she ate of the fruit of that tree (Genesis 3:5). She might have thought, "Well, that makes sense; I'd like to be like God." Women have a tendency to react emotionally in response to an unexpected event. Now, before I have all the women of the world hating me, may I use an illustration that may explain my reasoning?

When I was an active pastor, each year my wife and I would entertain the deacons of our church and their wives at a Christmas dinner at our home. Hors d'oeurves were served upstairs, and the main course was laid out in the basement. The basement was beautifully decorated for Christmas and the sumptuous meal was placed on a table at the foot of the stairs. There was a blazing fire in the open fireplace. It was a new home, and I had not had a chance to purchase a screen. Suddenly, without any warning, a squirrel that had been perched in our chimney getting warm, lost his footing and came crashing down into the flames and out into the room.

Faced with a burning fireball running wildly about, the women went wild. They scrambled for the only exit, the stairs, pushing, shoving, and jockeying to get out first. One lady raised her long skirt and climbed up on a chair to escape this menacing creature. I went through four years of Bible school and no one ever taught me how to put out a burning squirrel, but I knew one thing for sure. That was not the way to do it. The men could only watch and gawk; they had never seen such a display of emotion. When the commotion died down and the fire on the squirrel went out, the men put him in a box, and he was carried out and dumped in a snow bank. Now, admittedly, all women are not like that and these women would have acted differently had the event not been so sudden and caught everyone by surprise. But it remains that in a panic situation, the woman's first response is an emotional one. Just as Eve's initial response was an emotional one. "Do you mean to tell me that I would not have to die if

I just ate of the fruit of that tree? Let me at it!" (or words to that effect).

⪧ The Image Had to Be Restored ⪦

The image that was lost in the Garden had to be restored in order for man to continue to have a relationship with God. As Israel had taken on the image of an ox when she worshipped the golden calf, so we take on the image of those we worship (Psalm 106:20). Boys have their idols and pattern their lives after them. I heard of three girls who took their own lives after Marilyn Monroe died just to be with her in death. When humans sinned, no longer did we bear the image of God, but the imprint of Satan was upon us. We were truly the children of the devil (1 John 3:10). Not only did we change our image, but we changed the image of God to corruptible things such as men, birds, four-footed beasts, and creeping things (Romans 1:23). Man feels more comfortable worshipping a god on the same level as himself.

God's image is restored to mankind by Christ when they receive Him as their Savior. Kenneth Wuest in quoting John Lightfoot says, "The spiritual man in each believer's heart, like the primal man in the beginning of the world, was created after God's image . . . The new birth was a recreation in God's image; the subsequent life must be a deepening of this image thus stamped upon the man." Wuest continues, "This putting off of the old man and this putting on of the new man took place at the moment the Colossian sinner put his faith in Christ."[6] Every born-again believer has God's image recreated in him.

⇒ THIS IMAGE NEEDS DEVELOPING ⇒

This image, however, must be developed. No one is automatically a spiritually mature Christian when he is first saved; each is a newborn baby and must grow into a fully developed adult (1 Peter 2:2). The development is gradual. He is changed into the image of Christ from glory to glory (2 Corinthians 3:18). He is changed from one phase of glory to the next. When we learn all there is to learn on one level of glory, we pass on to the next level. When we learn how to serve as Jesus did when He washed the disciples' feet, we pass on to the next level of glory. When we can know the fellowship of His sufferings like Paul (Philippians 3:10), we can progress on to the next level of glory. When we practice self-denial like Jesus, who did not set limits, "even the death of the cross" (Philippians 2:8), we can pass to the next level of glory.

Chapter 11

My Struggle with Legalism

*I*t is much easier to be a legalist than to live by the principles of the Christian life. Legalism is vindictive, judgmental, unloving, and opinionated among a host of other negative traits. It practices those things Christians should avoid. I began my ministry with many of the traits of legalism. I judged people on the externals of dress, appearance, length of hair, kinds of music to which they listened, and whether religious leaders cooperated with liberals in religious services. Legalists sometimes seem to be more interested in "keeping the faith" than in helping sinners. Jesus said of legalists that "they bind heavy burdens and grievous to be borne, and lay them on men's shoulders; but they themselves will not move them with one of their fingers" (Matthew 23:4). Modern-day legalists expect other people to be bound by their own self-serving opinions rather than the plain teaching of the Word of God. They lift their opinions to the level of doctrine, giving them a false authority.

ᴈ∈ LEGALISM DEFINED ᴈ∈

Legalism is the belief that one is saved by the keeping of the law, or better, by one's exclusive opinion of the law. Modern-day legalists may believe that one is saved by faith in Christ, but they believe everyone must live the Christian life by their made-up set of rules. In addition to the primary definition of legalism [in which it refers to works of salvation] the term 'legalism' is commonly used to refer to the view that adherence to certain manmade rules is necessary for moral or spiritual righteousness and full acceptance and partnership in the Christian community. While rules are necessary for order in the Christian life, they are to be God's rules and not man's (Titus 2:11–12). By setting up his own rules, the modern-day legalist becomes authoritative about those rules and tends to give them the air of biblical authority. For example, he makes himself the guardian of "good" music. He becomes the sole judge of what is good music. He sets up rules for listening to the "right" music. If anyone disagrees with him, he is labeled a compromiser or an unspiritual person.

❂ A Stand Against Legalism ❂

Once I stood at a meeting and took exception to a petition offered for a vote criticizing a certain Christian university for its music. Three men, one of whom was the moderator, lashed out at me for voicing my opinion. I was amazed at such an outburst. There was no open forum with these men. Their opinions were the last word with no discussions allowed. Music, to me, is a matter of personal taste. Not all Christians agree that one style should fit all. I prefer traditional, but there is some beautiful contemporary I like. That does not mean that everybody should like what I like. I have good, Christian friends who love Southern Gospel, Blue Grass, Western, and contemporary. Who am I to tell them they are wrong? Music is not a doctrinal issue, but a cultural one and should be treated as such.

⇥ CHARACTER DETERMINES BEHAVIOR ⇤

Modern-day legalists appear to believe that one's behavior makes one's character, when, in reality, one's character determines one's behavior. What I do does not determine what I am, but what I am determines what I do. No one can categorize someone's character by one action. Abraham was not a liar because he lied about Sarah; God knew his character and called him the "Friend of God" (James 2:23). David was not an adulterer because he committed adultery with Bathsheba because God characterized him as ""a man after mine own heart" (Acts 13:22). Moses was not a murderer because he killed that Egyptian soldier. One act does not determine a man's character. Spread the lives of all three men out and pick out one word that would describe their whole life. It would not be liar, adulterer, or murderer. God never describes any of these three as such. No one action can describe a person's character. There is no scripture in the New Testament that condemns their characters as such.

Too many times, legalists judge people by their kind of music, their appearance, whether they are divorced or attend movie theaters. These things do not determine their character; their relationship with God is what determines their character. I realize Jesus said, "Ye shall know them by their fruits" (Matthew 7:16), but He was talking about false prophets (Matthew 7:15), not ordinary people. He had a message to ordinary people, however, when He said, "Judge not, that ye be not judged" (Matthew 7:1). We can know false prophets by their fruits, but we are not individually to judge others.

⋇ Looks Are Deceiving ⋇

We are not to judge others because we don't always know all the facts. A man had dental work done and was told to sit while the effects of the gas wore off. He forgot and left the office too soon. He became dizzy, began to stagger, and sat down on the curb to recover. A lady from his church saw him staggering and assumed he had been drinking. She gossiped to the whole church that she saw him drunk. She did not know all the facts. Some time ago, I received a call from a lady that she saw one of our deacons buying a lottery ticket. I asked him to explain, and he said he withdrew money from his bank's ATM machine, not a lottery machine. She did not know all the facts either.

⋇ Freed From Legalism ⋇

Jesus did not come to condemn the world (John 3:17a); He came that it might be saved (John 3:17b). If Jesus did not come to condemn the world, then what right does anyone else have to condemn it? His mission was to save the world, and we have the same mission: "As my Father hath sent me, even so send I you" (John 20:21). Are you saying that we should not preach against sin? No, we are told to preach the Word, and the Bible names sin. What I am saying is that we are not to judge people, no matter what their sins are, apart from the Word of God. On an individual basis, it is not our part to judge people's sin. Preach the Word and let the Word do the judging. We are told not to judge another man's servant (Romans 14:4), since he is accountable to his own master. The only one for whom an individual has to give an account is for himself (Romans 14:12).

⋙ Love Is The Answer ⋙

We are told not to judge one another, but to love one another. We cannot condemn, criticize, or judge those we love. The crux of spirituality is not outward actions, but it is "faith which worketh [expresses itself] by love" (Galatians 5:6). *Expressing itself* means superhuman power; faith, in and of itself, works with a superhuman power by love. It is not out of a sense of duty that we live godly lives, but out of love for the Savior. It is faith expressing itself through love that determines our behavior. Dennis Guernsey had it right when he said:

A person's ability to love is influenced, if not determined, by a person's psychological and relational history. If this is true in terms of our human relationships, why wouldn't it be true in terms of our relationship with God? To me, this is the key issue of spirituality, but in a very specific sense. For some, spirituality has to do with memorizing Scripture, reading the Bible, and praying daily—the spiritual disciplines. For others, it may involve the daily witness about faith in Jesus Christ as Lord. And to still others spirituality means an inward attitude of quiet reverence or self-sacrificial service to those around them. I define spirituality as "loving God." And when I talk about loving God, I mean the same kind of passionate, committed, or self-sacrificial love we can feel and demonstrate toward anyone else—whether a spouse, a child, or a friend. We have cause to love God because of who He is and because of what He has done for us, and He expects our love. [7]

Jesus said the first and great commandment was to love God with "all thy heart, and with all thy soul, and with all thy mind," and the second was to "love thy neighbor as thyself" (Matthew 22:37–39). He then made the astounding statement that "on these two commandments hang all the law and the prophets" (v. 40). In other words, the basis, or foundation, for the law and the prophets was to love God first and your neighbor second. We are never to judge God and our neighbor, but to love them. End of story.

Chapter 12

My Struggle with Showing Love

$\mathcal{W}$hen I was a child, parents did not express their love for their children. We knew they loved us, but it was not something that was expressed. They preferred to show their love by providing food, clothing, and shelter for us. They were very good to meet our needs, especially in the depression years in which I grew up, but to tell a child he was loved was just not done. The remains of the Victorian era in which perception was greater than substance was still in vogue. That is, to give the appearance of a happy family was much more important than actually meeting the emotional needs of the children. It wasn't enough to take for granted that I was loved. I yearned to hear the words, "I love you." Love is not just a feminine thing; boys like to hear it also.

Against this backdrop was my own hesitancy to express my love when I became a husband and a father. I married a wife who freely expressed her love, and later we had two wonderful daughters who did the same. With these three as my examples, I soon learned that I could express my love by working at it. I found that love was not just a feminine thing, but that men also could express their love without losing their manhood. In fact, I learned that expressing your love makes you a better man. I also found out that love is not just an emotional feeling (it is that, but so much more than that). It is an act of the will. That is the reason that Jesus said we are to love our enemies (Matthew 5:44). There is no way my emotions would allow me to love my enemies, but, if I am willing, I can *will* to love them. That is not a human thing, but a spiritual one. My humanity tells me I should get even with my enemies, not love them. Jesus wanted the world to know that only those who knew His Father could possibly do such a thing (Matthew 5:45).

⊃⊂ LOVE IS NOT JUST A FEELING ⊃⊂

One evening, my wife and I found ourselves at a dinner sitting across from two giddy teenage girls who were admiring all the boys as they came in. One girl, especially, kept using the word *love* in a flippant manner. "I just love his hair, his build, his height, etc." So I decided I would have a little fun, while at the same time teaching this girl a valuable lesson. I said to her, "You keep talking a lot about love. What is your definition of love?" She thought for a minute and replied, "It's a feeling you feel that you never felt before." Pretty good for a teenager, but totally wrong. To her, love was a feeling and nothing more. I said, "Let me see, one time I cut into a live electrical wire. I said to those around me that I was in love because I got a feeling that I never felt before. Or when I had the Asian flu while traveling, I got a feeling that I never felt before, so I said to my wife, 'Honey, I must be in love because I have a feeling that I never felt before.'" The girl grinned and said, "You're just being silly." I replied, "That may be so, but love is more than just a feeling; it is an act of the will."

The teenager's definition is what most people believe, that love is a feeling. Love songs, romantic novels, movies, and slick magazines all hype this concept. Most believe that love is an emotion only and it will last forever, but feelings wear out eventually. The commitment that one makes to love by one's own will is the enduring factor in marriage. Love is not the basis of marriage; commitment is. When that commitment is made, certain privileges come with it. The yielding of one's body to the other is one of those privileges. Outside of marriage, such privilege is not a privilege, but a sin (Acts 15:19–20).

While hope and faith are important, love is essential (1 Corinthians 13:8). It is by our love for each other that outsiders know we are followers of the Lord (John 13:35); it is love that distinguishes us from unbelievers (1 John 3:10), and it is love for our enemies that points us out as children of God (Matthew 5:44–45). If love were an emotion only, I would not love my enemies, but I would seek to get even for the way in which they had wronged me.

✳ THE BIBLICAL DEFINITION OF LOVE ✳

There are three words in the Greek for love: *eros*, *philos*, and *agape*. *Eros* is all physical love that takes and never gives. *Philos* is the highest form of human love possible. It gives but it expects to receive in return. It is love for a friend or love of country, but if it does not receive love in return, it will cease to love. *Agape* is the highest form of love that emanates from God and can only be practiced by His children (1 John 4:7–8). It gives unconditionally and expects nothing in return. This is the kind of love that God showed to the world (John 3:16) and husbands are to show to their wives (Ephesians 5:25).

Love is not a single item, but breaks up into thirteen different parts. No one can really say he loves until he has mastered all the different parts. Love can be compared to the parts of a watch. A watch is made up of different parts, yet it is a single unit. It could not operate until all parts are working properly. Neither can love operate fully until all parts are operating efficiently. For example, the first part of love, according to 1 Corinthians 13, is long-suffering, which means "long on self-control; self-restraint in the face of provocation which does not hastily retaliate nor promptly punish; it is the opposite of anger and is associated with mercy"[8] An incident in traffic taught me the meaning of "long on self-control; self-restraint in the face of provocation which does not hastily retaliate nor promptly punish." I had just read that definition in W. E. Vine's *Expository Dictionary of New Testament Words.* While still mulling these words over in my mind, I went to make a call on a church visitor from the Sunday before, and I made a wrong turn on a side street. I started to turn around, but I saw a van coming, and I pulled over to the curb, parked, and waited until he could pass. To my astonishment, the van was heading toward me, and, at the last instant, it swerved, barely missing me. I thought that strange, but I reasoned the driver must have had his attention diverted for a split second.

I didn't think anymore about it until after I turned my car around and saw the van at the corner with both doors open and two men with their hands on their hips waiting for you-know-who. I pulled up slowly, rolled my window down, and was greeted with these words, "You stupid idiot! You almost ran over me back there!" "Hello? I'm the stupid idiot? I was parked and you almost ran over me." And besides, I'm not stupid, I'm a college graduate. I'm six feet tall, weigh more than two hundred pounds and have muscles of steel. The man continued venting his rage by saying, "I ought to reach through this window, pull those glasses off, and punch you in the face." I had read just this morning that I am to be "long on self-control; self-restraint in the face of provocation which does not hastily retaliate nor promptly punish." Instead, I said, "Please forgive me; I'm sorry if I offended you," and drove off while he was still in a state of shock.

I must admit I had second thoughts later about what I would have done if he had stuck his hand in my window to punch me in the face. I would have rolled the window up on his arm, put the car in gear, attained a speed of sixty miles an hour, then rolled the window down and watched him roll. But I figured that was no way to practice love, so I happily drove back home rejoicing that I had done the spiritual thing. By the way, I never did make that call on the Sunday visitor.

Love is many more things. It does not envy (1 Corinthians 13:4); it does not vaunt itself (13:4), meaning it does not brag on itself; it is not swelled up with pride (13:4); it behaves itself appropriately at all times (13:5); it does not crave anything for itself, but thinks of others (13:5); it is not easily aroused to anger (13:5); it thinks no evil (13:5). Actually this is a bookkeeping term that means it does not keep a running account of things done against it. A typical example would be a husband is late picking his wife up from work because he was playing ball and forgot about her. She gets into the car and lambasts him with a tirade of angry words. He defends himself by reminding her of the incident last month when she smashed the right fender of the car backing out of the garage. Not to be outdone, she puts her computer brain to work and comes up with something he did several weeks ago that was offensive. Back and forth they go with things that happened months ago. We have a wonderful memory of wrongs done against us, but *agape* love does not keep a running account of things done against it. Instead, it forgives an infraction immediately and deletes it from its memory. It keeps a clean slate daily by forgiving each wrong as it happens.

The list of love's many attributes continues in 1 Corinthians. It is a rejoicer of truth (13:6), even if the truth incriminates itself. A husband who loves his wife will truthfully give an account of his whereabouts after any length of absence. Love is not resentful (13:7). Resentment is a "feeling back" to a time when you were done wrong. It is an emotional rehashing of some event in the past. Love chooses to capture those negative feelings of vengeance and replace them with a positive attitude of forgiveness. Loving one's enemies will not necessarily change the feelings of the enemy, but it has the wonderful effect of changing the offended one's outlook about the incident. He no longer allows bitterness and a vengeful spirit to control him, but he enjoys that wonderful, exhilarating, and calming effect of doing the right thing.

Love is neither opinionated nor arrogant and believes easily. It is hopeful (13:7); it believes God's purposes will be fulfilled in spite of the circumstances and it endures (13:7); nothing can defeat it. "Patient acquiescence, holding its ground when it can no longer believe nor hope."[9] Contrary to secular thought, love is not primarily physical. The physical aspect of love is a result, not a cause of love.

I now freely tell my wife, my two daughters, my grandchildren, and my ninety-nine-year-old mother that I love them. My mother, from her nursing home bed, is finally able to respond by saying, "I love you, too." I have waited for more than seventy years to hear those words, and I do enjoy hearing them.

Chapter 13

My Struggle with Trouble

*J*esus made three predictions that were certain to bring the disciples trouble unless they took precautions. An announcement of betrayal (John 13:21) was received with a mixture of unbelief, dismay, and self-examination. "Is it I?" (Mark 14:19) was the simultaneous outcry with which they questioned their own veracity. The subtlety of a betrayal was so beyond their thinking that they questioned their own motives. "Surely," they thought, "none of the others would betray Him. Am I being so self-deceived that it is really I?" Self-examination was the only sure way to determine who the culprit really was, they thought. But Jesus set their minds at ease by stating, "Let not your heart be troubled . . . ye believe in God, believe also in me" (John 14:1). It didn't matter who the betrayer was; they had no reason to be troubled by it. No matter what happened, they had Jesus to see them through. When we look at our surroundings, we are dismayed because we see no purposeful ending, but when we look to Jesus, we are encouraged because not only is there purpose, but there is meaning. There was purpose in His being betrayed—the means for getting Him to the cross. The meaning was (far above the heads of the disciples at this time) salvation for anyone who accepted His death as sufficient to atone for their sins. Salvation would be for anyone who would come to believe.

To be betrayed is a terrible thing, but to be betrayed by a friend is unthinkable. David, betrayed by Ahithophel, opined, "For it was not an enemy that reproached me; then I could have borne it: neither was it he that hated me that did magnify himself against me; then I would have hid myself from him: but it was thou, a man mine equal, my guide, and mine acquaintance. We took sweet counsel together, and walked unto the house of God in company" (Psalm 55:12–14). This was no ordinary friend, but a man who had counseled David through many battles, a man like himself (his peer), his companion and close friend. Ahithophel was a confidant with whom David revealed secrets unknown to others. Ahithophel's advice was as the Word of God to David (2 Samuel 16:23). But he was the grandfather of Bathsheba, with whom David had committed adultery. Instead of forgiving David, Ahithophel betrayed him.

Jesus looked upon Judas as a "friend" (Matthew 26:50), a close, intimate friend with whom He had shared His innermost sentiments, a friend He had trusted to be the treasurer of the group (John 12:6), a friend He allowed to be a part of His private world, and a friend to take His lifesaving message to the entire world. Judas endured the same hardships the other disciples did. ("Foxes have holes, and the birds of the air have nests; but the Son of man hath not where to lay his head" Matthew 8:20.) He suffered the same ridicule, preached the same message, and worked the same works (Matthew 10:5–8). He was chosen by the Lord (Matthew 10:4). You may ask, "What makes a man so blessed do such a terrible thing?" I wish I knew; all I know is he was a devil whom no one suspected (John 6:70). Ever know anyone like that? Sure you have. Betrayal by an intimate friend is the hardest to take.

I had such a friend who betrayed me. He had such a great potential as a preacher of the gospel. Every time he preached, he had the rapt attention of his hearers. Eyes were focused on his every movement, and ears were trained on his every word. His intellect was compelling, and his looks were appealing. His background as a pastor's son spoke well of his training. He sent out letters advertising his abilities in hopes of obtaining meetings in churches, but when no one responded, he turned to the business world, where his troubles began. Enthused at the prospect of becoming a very rich man, he made the terrible mistake of spending cash before he earned it and got himself in a mess of trouble. Unfortunately, he began to borrow money with the promise to pay everyone back, but he was never able to do that and filed for bankruptcy. I didn't have a lot of money, but I borrowed money to loan to him. During this time, I noticed a definite setback in his spiritual growth. Later, I learned he had become involved with women, other than his wife, and had started drinking. Sometime later he became so desperate for the notoriety that money brings, he robbed a bank and served nearly three years in prison. Why was he such a disappointment to me? He was my former son-in-law. What started out as a bright future turned out to be a wasted life. I had to lean hard on Jesus, who reminded me, "Let not your heart be troubled . . . ye believe in God, believe also in me" (John 14:1).

⋊⋉ These Predictions Could Apply To Us ⋊⋉

I had the same problem that I am sure the disciples had—anger instead of sorrow, bitterness instead of forgiveness, and finger-pointing instead of intercession. I had to remember that all of us are sinners and are capable of doing the same thing. Well, not exactly the same thing, but something just as bad. Paul accused the Romans of not only doing the same things as the heathen (such things as fornication, murder, hating God, boasting, etc.), but having pleasure in them that do them (Romans 1:29–32). I realize this is speaking of the heathen, but even the heathen know the judgment of God is against such things (Romans 1:32). I wonder if, in a way, we still hold to the ways of the heathen by judging someone by their actions rather than their character. David committed adultery, but does one act of adultery judge his entire life? The same is true of Abraham, who told a lie, and Moses, who killed a soldier. The fact that their acts are not repeated in the New Testament is evidence that God judged them by their character and not by their actions at the time. He knew what they would become and not what they were. Their potential was to be leaders and not washouts. He knew they had the desire to please Him above all else, and He could take that and form a character that others would follow. Again, we are reminded, "Let not your heart be troubled . . . ye believe in God, believe also in me" (John 14:1).

Not only were the disciples disappointed to learn that it was Judas who would betray Him, but the second prediction was nearly as bad—He would be leaving them. This meant a definite change in their circumstances. No one likes a change in his circumstances; most prefer the status quo. We feel comfortable in keeping things the same. When Jesus left, the disciples thought, "What will happen to us without a leader, and what about our ruling in His kingdom? Will there even be a kingdom if He leaves?" What they didn't realize was that God never changes our circumstances without having another positive purpose in mind. The disciples were still going to rule in Jesus' kingdom, but they needed to learn first that His kingdom was not like the kingdoms of the Gentiles, where the great exercise authority over the lesser. To be great in the kingdom of God, one must be like a servant (Matthew 20:25–28). It was necessary for Jesus to go away for them to learn this lesson by depending on the Holy Spirit to teach them (John 16:7).

Because He was going away, the disciples would do greater works than even He did (John 14:12). The greater works would be the three thousand souls who were saved on the day of Pentecost. They would experience greater power in prayer, "If ye shall ask any thing in my name, I will do it" (John 14:14). This is an open invitation to ask for anything (not just anything, but anything IN JESUS' NAME) and He will do it. That is, anything that promotes the name of Jesus, He will do it. They would come to know a greater Counselor, and He would be with them forever (John 14:16). They would experience a greater presence of God (John 14:18). Having Him inhabit their bodies was even better than His being physically present with them. They would receive a greater understanding. The Holy Spirit would be their

Teacher to remind them of what Jesus had said unto them (John 14:26). He would give them a greater peace, not as the world gives, but as a legacy that comes from the Son of God (John 14:27).

My younger daughter came down with diabetes when she was nine years old. We were devastated, to say the least. As I related earlier, she woke up one morning about 3:00 A.M. complaining that she couldn't breathe. I called her doctor, and he said to put her in the shower with steam and the steam would free her to breathe. We had previously taken her to this same doctor with symptoms of diabetes, but he assured us that was not the case—she did not have diabetes. I put her in the shower, but it didn't help. I called the hospital, and they said to bring her in. The doctor there said I got her in just before she went into a coma. The next few days were critical, but she pulled through and has lived a rather normal life except for times of insulin shock that required trips back to the hospital. She is now in her fifties and, except for the loss of sight in her right eye, is fairly normal. She is our pastor's wife and enjoying every minute of it.

Our circumstances changed drastically. A new menu was established for the whole family because we didn't want to point her out as different. The whole family was healthier as a result. I took her on a date one night (before those awful boys had a chance to date her) and told her she was blessed because the Lord had trusted her with suffering that we could never know. He would see to it that this, too, would honor Him and bring glory to His name because she was called according to His purpose (Romans 8:28). Again, we were reminded of the words of our Lord, "Let not your heart be troubled . . . ye believe in God, believe also in me" (John 14:1). Our God is greater than our circumstances. But my wife and I did not get victory immediately. I became anxious. Anxiety is to be afraid of what *might* happen; fear is to be afraid of what is actually happening. Fear is going into the woods and being immediately confronted by a bear; anxiety is going into the woods and being afraid that you *might* be confronted by a bear. I was afraid of what *might* happen to my little girl. Every time I closed my eyes, I could see her body in a casket. It was horrible. This continued for about six weeks when it dawned upon me that the Lord had said, "Let not your heart be troubled . . . ye believe in God, believe also in me" (John 14:1). I finally acquiesced to the will of God. I find it impossible to declare the peace that followed. I began to sleep again, the world was fresh and green again, and life was again really worth living.

Jesus' next prediction really shook the disciples up—that Peter would actually deny the Lord. They knew he was rambunctious, but it was beyond the realm of belief that he could deny the Lord. As the leader, he was allowed to accompany the Lord to the Mount of Transfiguration. There he saw the glory of the Lord shine forth in its brightness with all its splendor thereof (Matthew 17:2). It was Peter who defended the Lord in the Garden, took up the sword, and cut off the ear of Malchus (John 18:10). But apparently, Peter returned to his old self and became fearful for his life. What would cause this staid, faithful warrior of the faith to disallow he ever knew Him?

Could it be that Peter became too self-confident? He bragged he would lay down his life for Him (John 13:37). On one occasion he even said, "Even if all fall away on account of you, I never will" (Matthew 26:33 NIV). He had need of Paul's words in Romans 12:3: "Do not think of yourself more highly that you ought, but rather think of yourself with sober judgment" (NIV). Could it have been that Peter would have been humiliated by the Lord's death? He vehemently objected when the Lord told him of His death, "Never, Lord! . . . This shall never happen to you!" (Matthew 16:22 NIV). Is it possible that—since Peter had preached everywhere that Jesus was the Messiah, which was thought to mean He would be the conquering hero who would liberate Israel from the heel of the Roman boot—Peter was fearful of shame? For Jesus to die meant that He had failed. Could that have been the reason Peter exclaimed, "I don't know the man!" (Matthew 26:74 NIV)?

Whatever the reason, it was evident that Peter had failed miserably. A man came into my office one day with a sad face. It was evident that something awful was bothering him. His story unwound as follows: he was a member of my church in good standing, but he considered himself a failure. I asked him why, and he told me he had a problem with alcohol. He had a good job and a wonderful family, but every so often, he would lose it and go on a binge. He kept saying he was a failure. He had failed his family, his friends, and his fellow workers. In desperation he came to me. In desperation

I quickly searched for an answer when all of a sudden, there it was. The Holy Spirit came to my rescue. I said, "You know, the Lord had a choice when He created you. He could have said, 'I don't think I will create _____ because I know in the future he will mess up.' But He didn't say that. He said instead, 'I will create _____ because I know that even though he will mess up, I will show him My mercy and forgive him, knowing he will trust Me to not let it happen again.'"

God could have said the same about David, Abraham, and Moses, but He didn't because He knew what they would become. Satan condemns us for our actions. To him, one act of adultery means you are an adulterer; one lie and you are a liar; one murder and you are a murderer. The list of characteristics of the wicked found in Revelation 21:8 states that all liars shall have their part in the lake that burns with fire and brimstone. Let me ask you whether you have told a lie. We all have, but does that mean we will all burn in the lake of fire and brimstone? Not if you know the Lord Jesus, you won't. It simply means that those characteristics were *a way of life*. The wicked's way of living was to be fearful, unbelieving, abominable, murderers, whoremongers, sorcerers, etc. They were that way because they chose that way of life. These things are their character traits; they act according to what each character trait dictates. They cannot be any other way. They are, by nature, that way.

Peter failed miserably, but so did Abraham, Moses, and David. I showed the man who came to me that though Abraham lied about Sarah, lying did not characterize his life. If you were to spread the whole life of Abraham out to view in total, lying would not characterize him; it would be only one incident in many. God forgives sin in the life of His saints because He knows they have the potential to overcome that weakness and learn from their mistakes. Character is not based on what individuals do, but on what they will become. The New Testament does not mention the sins of the Old Testament saints, which means God forgave them. Peter went on to open the door to the Gentiles to be saved. He preached a message that won three thousand souls (Acts 2:41). He became a leader of the early church, and he will someday sit on a throne with Jesus judging the twelve tribes of Israel (Matthew 19:28). That's pretty good for someone who denied he ever knew Christ. No, Jesus forgives sin and forgives it completely.

❧ Keep On Believing in Jesus ❧

I, too, failed my Lord and my wife. I left the Lord out of my thinking to do my own thing. I allowed my focus to be on things that were sinful. I wrongfully thought I had the freedom to do my own thing. The results were disastrous. My relationship with the Lord was broken. I would go through the motions of having devotions, but with no power in my life. I lived a life of misery, trouble, and turmoil until I broke down in tears and confessed to the Lord and my wife what I had been doing. I found out at that time what a wonderful Lord I had—One who would accept me back into fellowship and forgive my terrible sin. My wife also forgave me and accepted me back with open arms. I also found the words of the Lord Jesus to be precious and true, "Let not you

heart be troubled . . . ye believe in God, believe also in me"
(John 14:1).

Chapter 14

My Struggle with Old Age

*J*okes about old age do not make it any easier to get older. You know you're old when: somebody admires your alligator shoes and you're barefoot. Or you sit in a rocking chair and can't get it going. Or you sink your teeth into a steak and they stay there. As you age, you realize that your stay on earth is getting shorter. I know that Christians are to look at aging as bringing them that much closer to going home, but every Christian has a human side and wonders about (and dreads) whether suffering will accompany his death.

A solution for that is not to think about dying, but to hope for the Lord's return. When the Lord was taken into heaven, the angels told the disciples to quit gazing into heaven because the Lord would return the same way He went into heaven (Acts 1:11). They were to get busy with their mission on earth while looking for His imminent return. I believe it is our responsibility as Christians to accomplish as much as possible as long as we live, while looking for the Lord's imminent return.

❧ BEARING FRUIT IN OLD AGE ❧

The older I get, the more I realize I don't have a lot of time left, and there is much to be done before the Lord returns. Most of us have been programmed to think that retirement is a time to quit everything and take a well-deserved rest. Dr. Frank Crane takes a different view. He states, "Because of the remarkable advances by modern science, the average lifespan is lengthening. Millions of folks past 65 are now living in enforced idleness by the political doctrine that a man is on the shelf when he happens to celebrate his 65th birthday. The doctrine is definitely not scientific. You are never on the shelf until you put yourself there."[10] Too many people put themselves on the shelf prematurely. The psalmist gives hope to the aged by stating, "They will still bear fruit in old age, they will stay fresh and green" (Psalm 92:14 NIV).

❊ Accomplishments Of Old Age ❊

Old age is the time for which God has been preparing us in our prior years. It is a time when wisdom and understanding are attained. "Is not wisdom found among the aged? Does not long life bring understanding?" (Job 12:12 NIV). Unfortunately, for a time I took the easy attitude about old-age and rested in my retirement, but now I look at it with the poet as a time to "bloom before the face of God."

> *I shall not mind*
> *The whiteness of my hair,*
> *Or that slow steps falter*
> *On the stair,*
> *Or that young friends hurry*
> *As they pass,*
> *Or what strange image*
> *Greets me in the glass—If I can feel,*

As roots feel in the sod,

That I am growing old to bloom

Before the face of God."[11]

Some of the accomplishments of older men are phenomenal. "Between the ages of 70 and 83 Commodore Vanderbilt added about 100 million to his fortune. Kant at 74 wrote his 'Anthropology, Metaphysics of Ethics and Strife of the Faculties.' Tintoretto at 74 painted the vast Paradise canvas 74 feet by 30. Verdi at 74 produced his masterpiece 'Othello'; at 80, 'Falstaff' and at 85 the famous 'Ave Maria,' 'Stabat Mater,' and 'Te Deum.' Lamarck at 78 completed his great zoological work, 'The Natural History of the Invertebrates.' Oliver Wendell Holmes at 79 wrote 'Over the Teacups.' Cato at 80 began the study of Greek. Goethe at 80 completed 'Faust.' Tennyson at 83 wrote 'Crossing the Bar'; Titian at 98 painted his historic picture of the 'Battle of Lepanto.'"[12]

It is reported that George Muller said, "Let it be our unceasing prayer that as we grow older we may not grow colder in the ways of God." He lived into his late nineties and had written long before, "As we advance in years, let us not decline in spiritual power; but let us see to it that an increase of spiritual vigor and energy be found in us, that our last days may be our best days . . . Let the remaining days of our earthly pilgrimage be spent in an ever-increasing, earnest consecration to God."[13]

Most of us at age eighty are looking to spend most of our time in the rocking chair, but it was at that age that Moses was called to lead the children of Israel out of Egypt. For the next forty years of his life, he played nursemaid to more than two million Jewish malcontents, but was successful in standing up to Pharaoh and getting his people out of slavery and into the Promised Land. None of us at more than ninety years of age would be able to face ferocious lions in their own den, but Daniel did and lived to tell his story. It was said of Caleb that he was as strong at eighty-five as he was the day Moses sent him to spy out the land forty-five years earlier (Joshua 14:10–11). These men and others proved the principle in Proverbs 16:31 (NIV) "Gray hair is a crown of splendor; it is attained by a righteous life."

George Müller lived such a righteous life and, though physically fragile, began an evangelistic tour at the age of seventy lasting for seventeen years which amounted to travel equivalent to eight times around the world. As a young man, he had serious and frequent illnesses, which disqualified him for military duty and many predicted his early death. Yet he is quoted as saying at ninety-two, "I have been able, every day and all the day, to work, and with that ease as seventy years ago." He ascribed his longevity to three causes: [1] "The exercising himself to have always a conscience void of offense, both toward God and toward men. [2] To the love he felt for the Scriptures, and the constant recuperative power they exercised upon his whole being (Proverbs 4:20). [3] To the happiness he felt in God and His work, which relieved him of all anxiety and needless wear and tear in his labors."[14] Some, unfortunately, have traded off righteousness for pleasure and have lost their productivity and purpose for all their prior years. Paul laments that Demas was such a man, "For

Demas, because he loved this world, has deserted me and has gone to Thessalonica" (2 Timothy 4:10 NIV).

It is just not true that our most productive years happened when we were younger. Some researchers have looked into the histories of about four hundred famous men and found that 66 percent of the world's greatest work has been done by men past sixty. They found of the group's greatest achievements, "35 per cent came when the men were between 60 and 70; 23 percent when they were between 70 and 80; and 8 percent when they were more than 80."[15] Some excuse themselves by stating they cannot learn like they could when they were younger. That theory is rejected by most educators who, along with Milford F. Henkel, Ph.D., believe, "The adult can learn as easily as the child. In fact, there are certain factors that often make it easier for the adult to learn than the child . . . Adults often simplify the learning process concerning the things they know. It's easy to walk or talk after you know how, but not *while* you are learning how . . . If an adult realizes that learning and the ability to learn do not stop at childhood but continues throughout life, he can develop an attitude of continuous learning."[16] I am amazed how senior citizens sit around all day and do nothing when there is a whole world to discover. Granted, some are physically handicapped. If their minds are sharp, however, they could use the Internet to learn all kinds of interesting things. I told of my bout with vertigo and how it took trips to four doctors to find the cause of my problem. The third doctor found excess fluid in my inner ear, but did very little to treat it. I became frustrated and researched the Internet to find that the vestibular nerve could cause such problems. I looked up an etiologist (one who specializes in finding causes of diseases) and am now being properly treated for my problem. Had I been like some older persons, I would have done nothing and suffered. The point is to keep on learning, exploring, discovering new things no matter how old we become. The Bible is full of new and fresh things for us to discover each day. Someone has wisely said, "Never count how many years you have, but how many interests you have." Years do not matter so long as your interests are active.

ᴐᴄ A BLESSED FUTURE AWAITS ᴐᴄ

The future is much brighter for the Christian than the unbeliever. The Christian will live for a thousand years on this earth where there will be no crime, no sin, no sickness, and no growing old. It is called the Millennium and will be a time when the Lord Jesus will be in full control (Revelation 20:4–6). Peace will be the order of the day, and everybody will have something to do. Jesus will be worshipped, adored, and glorified. All races, tribes, genders, and tongues will get along with each other without bickering or fighting. It will be a glorious time of supreme gladness, hope, and joy. Satan and his cohorts will be bound during this entire time (Revelation 20:1–3). The martyrs for Christ and all the righteous dead will reign with Christ (Revelation 20:4–6). So what does it matter about the measly seventy-plus years during this lifetime? We have a much better and much longer life coming: "He who testifies to these things says, 'Yes, I am coming soon.' Amen. Come, Lord Jesus" (Revelation 22:20 NIV).

Chapter 15

My Struggle with Suffering Wrongfully

*I*t is only human that when I do something wrong I get punished for it, but it has never made any sense at all to be punished for something I did not do. Yet that is exactly what the Lord would have us do. He wants me to act spiritually and not humanly. Most of us grew up with the idea that every bad incident deserved a response to even the score. "You hit me, I hit you back," was the only fair response. Jesus changed all that, however, when He said through the apostle Paul, "Vengeance is mine; I will repay, saith the Lord" (Romans 12:19).

It is only human to take personal vengeance. It feels good to even a score. A sense of satisfaction comes in like a flood when I "make things right." After the initial euphoric moment, however, there follows the emptiness of wondering if I did the right thing. The Bible explains the emptiness. Vengeance belongs to God and when you take personal vengeance, you take something that belongs to Him. He reserves the right to take vengeance for Himself (Romans 12:19).

He does this for several reasons. By my taking personal vengeance myself, I have robbed Him of showing Himself strong by letting Him handle the situation. By handling the situation myself, I have not brought closure to the situation because the other party will inevitably try and get even with me. And finally, I will never learn the most vitally important lesson of suffering wrongfully. Suffering wrongfully is to be willing to overlook wrongful treatment from another person and continue loving that person anyway.

In my forty-three years of counseling, I have found the greatest problem to be the unwillingness to forgive one who has wronged the other. A relative, a friend, or a business partner has done wrong, and the offended one desires to get even. Anger, bitterness, and hatred creep in and leave the offended one with a problem. The solution to the problem is simple: overlook wrongful treatment from another person and continue loving that person anyway. In other words, be willing to suffer wrongfully.

✠ THE TEST BEGINS ✠

While I was writing this chapter, an incident happened that would test whether I would be willing to suffer wrongfully. A very close family member, who depends upon my wife and me to drive her places, called early in the morning to ask when my wife would pick her up that day and take her to the department store. I was ashamed to tell her we were still in bed, so I promised to call back later to give a time she would be picked up. When I called back, she was "hopping mad" and immediately began to accuse us of not caring about her schedule, of being disrespectful and selfish. My first reaction was to feel terribly hurt; after all, I felt I had done nothing to deserve such an outburst. The first knee-jerk reaction is almost always an emotional one. The fact that our personality consists of one-third emotion may contribute to the problem. I certainly was not in control of my spirit at this point. "He that hath no rule over his own spirit is like a city that is broken down, and without walls" (Proverbs 25:28).

My second reaction was to defend my wife and me against such outlandish false accusations. It was not true that we had been disrespectful; we did care about her schedule and we did not believe we were being selfish. After all, my wife was ready to walk out the door and pick her up at that very moment. The truth was that we loved her very much and were glad to transport her whenever and wherever she wanted. My third reaction stemmed more from anger than love. I decided I would have nothing to do with her in the future. She had said during her tirade that she had gotten along without us in the past, and she did not need us now. I knew that was not true because we were her only means of support. *Well,* I thought, *let's just see how well she can get along without us; we just won't have anything to do with her from now on.* But, of course, all these were sinful reactions. More later.

Peter thought he was doing right when he took up a sword and cut off the ear of Malchus, until Jesus said, "Put up again thy sword into his place: for all they that take the sword shall perish with the sword" (Matthew 26:52). This rebuke to Peter was intended to teach that those who live violently will die violently. In other words, "Whatsoever a man soweth, that shall he also reap" (Galatians 6:7). Jesus was saying to Peter that he was not to be like those who live by the sword, but by a higher standard. That standard was to suffer wrongfully, which Peter had learned by the time he wrote his epistle.

In 1 Peter 2:19–20 he wrote, "For this is thankworthy, if a man for conscience toward God endure grief, suffering wrongfully. For what glory is it, if, when ye be buffeted for your faults, ye shall take it patiently? but if, when ye do well, and suffer for it, ye take it patiently, this is acceptable with God." He had learned his lesson well. Most Christians have not yet learned this because it is only practiced by the spiritually mature. You will allow suffering you feel is necessary. You undergo the pain of major surgery to correct your affliction; brave men go off to war and undergo the rigors of fighting to stop their enemies, and musicians endure the agony of many hours of practice to be the very best. In the same way, Christians are more than glad to suffer persecution that advances the cause of Christ. However, they renege when the suffering has no apparent reason, and they complain that it isn't fair.

✺ Suffering Always Has a Purpose ✺

It was not fair for the Lord Jesus to suffer even though He was innocent of any wrongdoing. What was fair about Paul's suffering for the sake of the gospel and Job's suffering though he was guiltless? If only, as I go through these times of suffering wrongfully, I could see purpose, I know I would understand, but knowing there is purpose is all I need to know. Jesus knew His purpose was to die that others might live. Paul was willing to suffer for the gospel's sake. As far as we know, Job never knew the purpose for his suffering, but he knew there was purpose. Otherwise, how could he say, "The LORD gave, and the LORD hath taken away; blessed be the name of the LORD" (Job 1:21)? Only one with an implicit faith that God knew what He was doing could make such a statement.

Peter told me not to think it strange when I go through suffering, but to rejoice because I am a partaker of Christ's sufferings (1 Peter 4:12–13). The purpose of my sufferings is not for my sins, but for my identification with Jesus Christ. He said, "If the world hate you, ye know it hated me before it hated you . . . If they have persecuted me, they will also persecute you" (John 15:18, 20). Knowing that my suffering is because of my identification with Christ is all the purpose I need.

To suffer wrongfully is an opportunity to show others that I am not like other people. For example, slaves who were Christians would react the same way toward their masters whether they were good and gentle or forward (mean, averse) (1 Peter 2:18). Pagan slaves would react to a mean master in a rebellious and mean-spirited way, but not a Christian slave. This strong testimony would bring their masters under conviction of sin. This is the reason that Jesus said to "love your enemies" (Matthew 5:44) that "ye may be [known as] the children of your Father which is in heaven" (Matthew 5:45). This unconventional action might be the means of persuading some into the kingdom of God. "If they can act that way, there might be something to this Christianity after all," the unsaved might reason.

To act in such a manner would need a purpose other than people being brought under conviction of sin. There is something within you that demands that every wrong must be made right. Wrong is a negative that must have a positive to maintain a balance. God provides that perfect balance when He says, "For conscience toward God" (1 Peter 2:19). You can endure grief and suffer wrongfully because you have a desire to please God and you know this pleases Him because He says such action is "thankworthy" (1 Peter 2:19). Kenneth S. Wuest says, "The Greek word translated, 'thank worthy,' refer[s] to an action which is beyond the ordinary course of what might be expected and therefore commendable."[17] God is pleased when we suffer wrongfully. He is pleased because you are letting Him be your defender. Nothing pleases Him more than when you put aside your emotions of anger, hatred, and bitterness and leave to Him how He will work things out. You get out of His way so He can do His work. Romans 12:19 says you are to set aside your desire to get even and give place to His wrath so He will be able to work. I remember years ago that my assistant pastor, Les Ollila, used to tell abused wives to get out of the way and let God hit their husbands. In this way, they were giving place to God's wrath. Getting even makes sense to our human natures, and it feels good at the time, but believers now have spiritual natures. Acting according to our human natures only brings frustration and guilty consciences.

⇥ A BETTER WAY ⇤

To finish my story about my family member, that evening, my wife prepared one of her favorite dishes (apple crisp); I cooked an extra hamburger on the grill. With these gifts in hand, we went over that evening. To our surprise, she greeted us with a smile. We stayed and talked for a while, and my wife made arrangements to pick her up the next day to take her to the department store and everything turned out great. That was not easy for us to humble ourselves before such an outrageousness display of childishness, but matters would have gotten worse had we given a normal response. In assessing the situation later, I wondered if she had acted badly because she craved our attention and, because of our busyness, we had failed to give it.

Chapter 16

My Struggle with My Dad

*H*e wasn't much in the eyes of some people, but to me he was MY DAD. It was true that he cheated on my mother, lived a wild life, and became a hopeless alcoholic (we called it "drunkard" in my day), but he was still MY DAD. No amount of persuasion from my mother, my aunts, cousins, and a host of other relatives could deter me from loving MY DAD. He was truly a Dr. Jekyll and Mr. Hyde type. Sober, he was the most tender, most loving and sensitive human being one could ever hope to know. Drunk, he became a wild man. I still remember the two places he and my mother took me when they went dancing. The first was a respectable dance hall attended by normal, peace-loving people. The other was a roadhouse frequented by the other crowd. At the one he was sober and acted the perfect gentleman, and at the other he was like a wild lion let loose from captivity.

I still cherish the one time he picked me up in his arms and lovingly danced me around the dance floor (at the respectable place) and proudly showed me off to all the adults. It was a high time for me that forever etched itself in my memory. There was no feeling like being held by a big, six-foot, two-hundred-pound strapping and strong daddy who seemed so proud to have me as his son. On the other hand, at the roadhouse I was never allowed inside. I stayed outside and played with the other kids.

Inevitably, one of the kids yelled, "Look, a fight!" and all the kids went running to the long steps leading into the road-house where two men were flailing away at each other while tumbling outside and rolling down the steps, that is, all but me. One of the kids asked, "Aren't you coming?" I answered in a know-it-all manner, "No, it's my dad." It was no big deal to me because it happened every time. I never knew what led to the fight until my mother later filled me in on the details. My dad was the life of the party, joking with the other patrons and having a great old time; that is, until he got boozed up and started becoming boisterous and annoying, which brought the manager to try and calm him down. He tried gentle persuasion and tried every way to settle this out-of-control brute peacefully, but my dad would have none of that and started swinging at the manager. To defend himself, the manager swung back, which became a full-blown fight and led to their exit outside and down the long set of stairs. But even this could not change my mind about my dad. I still proudly claimed him as MY DAD. I even bragged to my school pals about his great fighting ability.

The next day, true to form, he would put me in the car and drive out to the roadhouse and sheepishly approach the manager and apologize profusely for his behavior from the night before. But here's the good part; he would always buy a red soda pop for me before he began his conversation. I really never knew why this same scenario took place each time except maybe it was his way of proving to the manager he was genuinely sorry by purchasing something from him. Some sort of a peace offering? I could never figure it out, but I was so glad to receive it, I never spent much time trying.

He never had a fight unless he drank, and when he drank, his fighting was inevitable. On one occasion, he tried to drag my mother from a car, but she refused. She knew he was drunk and just wanted to stay in the car out of his way. This angered him, and he grabbed her leg and began pulling. I believe a group of men and women had been out partying with them, and they were standing outside the car witnessing my dad's violent behavior. Suddenly, several of the men intervened and beat my dad to a frazzle. Someone must have taken me from the scene because I never saw any of this happen. Because of my young age, they probably thought I should not be witnessing such a violent event. I was told about it later. I only remember being escorted to our upstairs apartment and into the kitchen where I watched my mother gently cleaning my dad's bloody face with a love worthy of the noblest saint. I felt remorse and great sadness for my dad, and I felt bad for how he treated my mother, but through it all he was still MY DAD.

He was a burly man and strong as an elephant. I was told that one time the police were called because of his drunken and violent behavior, but the three officers could not subdue him enough to get him into the squad car, so they left without him. In spite of his violent temper and raucous behavior, I never feared him.

In my childish innocence I only knew I loved him. This showed itself one time when my mother and I were staying with my aunt (by then my parents were separated), and

I heard my aunt scream that my dad was coming up the sidewalk to the house and he was drunk. There was terror in the house. My aunt, uncle, and three cousins were huddled around each other, fearing the worst. I remember inching myself through this crowd at the front door, quickly slipping out on the front porch, and running down the stairs and toward my dad. I heard my aunt gasp at the scene, and someone called out, "Bobby, come back!" But there was no stopping me because I did not see what they saw. They saw an angry, drunken man, hell-bent to hurt someone, but I saw MY DAD whom I loved very much. To everyone's amazement he smiled, picked me up, and hugged me. Oh, that felt so good to this young upstart to know his dad really loved him. After a short while, he put me down and walked away without uttering a word. I was welcomed back into the house to a very relieved group.

When the Japanese attacked Pearl Harbor in 1941, the lives of all Americans were changed. The draft became a reality, and young men were either drafted into the armed services or patriotically volunteered to serve. My dad was beyond the draft age at this time, but, because of his patriotism, wanted to serve in some way. He ended up working in a shipyard in Newport News, Virginia, building ships for the navy. I visited him there one summer for a month. While I was there, he got drunk, ran a stop sign, and rammed another car. That accident resulted in several bodily injuries. I felt bad for the injured, but I excused my dad's behavior because, after all, he was still MY DAD.

In typical macho fashion he hid his feelings from every-body including me. However, he slipped up when I got ready to leave and go back home. He took me to the railroad station and told me good-bye, but when he turned to leave, I got a glimpse of a tear trickling down his cheek. Again, I was proud that he was MY DAD.

✂ CIRCUMSTANCES CHANGED, BUT NOT DAD ✂

After the war, he came back to our home city to live. By this time, he had a new wife, my stepmother, whom I loved very much, and eventually three children. But even though he had another family, he was still MY DAD, and I loved him as much as ever. He made me proud by attending my football games and cheering for me. I was even more proud of him because he sat with my new stepdad, whom I also loved very much. After the games, he would always give me instructions on how to play my position, even though he had never played a game of football in his life. He was still MY DAD.

I understood because he was a perfectionist. "If you plan on doing something, do it to the best of your ability" was his motto. In his work as a sheet metal worker and welder, this was his philosophy. One time the city water department asked him to weld a metal box that would hold water with no leaks whatsoever. It seemed that several attempts had been made with no success before they came to him. He did it on his first attempt. That was MY DAD.

He enjoyed agitating people immensely. A lady who grew up with him told me if someone were to remark about a white horse walking down the street, my dad would swear it was a black horse. I remember once, he and my uncle were discussing politics, and my uncle was berating the communists. Even though everybody knew my dad was against communism, he took the other side and said how wonderful communism was for the people. True to form, that was MY DAD.

⊰ A CHANGED DAD ⊱

I knew my dad was not saved, but I never gave up in witnessing to him and praying for him. I was a young preacher boy and eager to preach somewhere. My chance came when a pastor asked another preacher boy and me to preach a youth revival at his church. We would alternate nights in preaching. My stepmother saw to it my dad was at every service. The meetings went on for a whole week, but there was no movement by my dad. Finally, the week was up with good results, but my dad still refused to get saved. The pastor and deacons thought the meetings were going so well, they extended the revival on a night-to-night basis. My friend preached the first night, but still no movement from my dad. It was my turn next, and I preached a simple gospel message. The invitation was given, and the very first person down the aisle was MY DAD. My prayers were answered. There he was, a six-foot, two-hundred-pound man who was not afraid of anybody, standing there crying like a baby. I was never more proud of MY DAD than at that very moment.

Old things had passed away, and everything had become new in my dad's life. No more drinking, no more swearing, no more infidelity; he was truly a new creature in Christ.

The Lord had done what Alcoholics Anonymous could not do. Though they are a good work and help many people, they could not help my dad. He was totally unable to help himself; he could only throw himself on the mercy of God.

His life changed immensely. He refused to shop in grocery stores that sold alcoholic beverages. He stopped smoking immediately, and his language cleaned up overnight. He became a man of prayer and sought to know the Bible like never before.

Finally, his old life caught up with him, and in 1983 he suffered a stroke that would eventually take his life. In the hospital he witnessed to his old friends who came to see him. They never came back. He had become a man of faith, and they could not understand that. In June of 1984, he made his entrance into heaven, leaving behind a legacy with his four children, who could truly say of him, "He's MY DAD."

Chapter 17

My Struggle with Deathbed Experiences

*O*ne of the most difficult duties for me as a pastor was to visit the unsaved friends or relatives of my people for the purpose of trying to win them to Jesus Christ. All kinds of excuses would pop into my head as to why I should be the one saddled with such an awesome task. I would think, "Why didn't they witness to this person when he was well and save me the trouble of having to do it now?" or, "How do they expect me to witness to someone who does not even know me?" or "What if they are in a coma or something? It would be just another wasted trip." If these excuses did not convince me not to go, I had others. "I don't have the time," "I am needed in other places," or "There are other more important calls for me to make" were my backup excuses. To top it all off, I felt uneasy about the prospect of going into a hospital room and witnessing to a patient with two or three other roommates listening in. However, when it came time to go, I always went and was glad I did. Some of my most rewarding experiences occurred because I made these calls.

✄ NURSES TO THE RESCUE ✄

It was a warm spring afternoon when I walked into the room of an older man who was not expected to live much longer. I had prepared myself beforehand by convincing myself that no matter what was about to happen, I was going to witness to this man. I was psyched up and ready to go (no matter how many roommates he might have). But when I arrived, he was sound asleep, and his wife was faithfully seated beside his bed and ready to serve his needs when he awoke. I thought, "Now what do I do? If I wake him up, he will probably be in a grouchy mood, but if I let him sleep, it would be a wasted trip." I had just enough time to introduce myself to his wife when two nurses walked in and announced it was time to change his sheets, and they promptly woke him up. They asked his wife and me to step outside during the process, which gave me the opportunity to explain to the wife the purpose of my visit. I began by asking the religious background of her husband and found out he had none, although she said he had read the Bible through six times and was a very good man. I explained that being good never got anyone into heaven, and, with her permission, I would like to explain to her husband how he could know he would go to heaven when he died. She consented, and we were called back into the room.

This time I encountered a wide-awake patient because, in addition to making his bed, the nurses had given him a bath. I started out by introducing myself and made small talk to put him at ease. Then I told him his wife had told me he had read the Bible through six times, and his face lit up. I could tell he was very proud of that feat. Then I asked if, in his reading, he had discovered how to get to heaven. This made him a little uneasy because he said, "You need to talk to my wife about that kind of thing." I replied, "I already talked to your wife in the hall, and she said it was all right for me to talk to you about how you can know you are going to heaven when you die." Well, that stopped him in his tracks, and he agreed to listen to me.

I explained that reading the Bible was good, but it does no good unless you apply the things you read. I explained that the religious leaders of Jesus' day knew the Scriptures, but that He told them they needed to know Him because the Scriptures were all about Him. I then explained the Romans Road to him and asked him if he would like to give himself to Jesus and allow Him to become his Savior. The man consented and, in childlike manner, submitted himself to Jesus Christ. His countenance changed immediately, and his wife was elated. He died shortly thereafter. By the way, I can't remember whether he had any roommates. He may have had one in the four-bed room, but I was oblivious to his presence, thanks to the Holy Spirit.

⋋ A Dying Father ⋌

On another occasion, I found myself in the hospital room of the dying father of one of my faithful laymen. The dying man's wife and daughter, who were seated at the foot of his bed, tended to him. He was on a respirator and unable to speak. I talked mainly to the wife and told her why I had come. She seemed receptive, even though the family was of a different religion than I represented. Her son had told me they were very strict in their religion, believing theirs was the only true religion. I spent some time discussing her husband's condition, and she told me in a whisper that he did not have much time left. I then went to the bedside of the patient, identified myself, and announced that I had come to tell him how to know he would go to heaven someday. I did not say "when he died," because he was so near death.

I took his hand and asked him to answer my questions by squeezing my hand once for "yes" and twice for "no." I asked him if he understood, and he squeezed my hand once. Yes, he understood. I explained to him that the Bible makes it very clear that one must be saved before he could go to heaven. I asked him if he were familiar with the term *saved*, and if he had ever been saved. He squeezed my hand, "No." I asked him if he would allow me to explain what it meant to be saved. He squeezed my hand, "Yes." I then very slowly proceeded to give him the Romans Road, explaining that he was a sinner (Romans 3:10), and the price to pay for sin is death (Romans 6:23), that Jesus had already paid the price (Romans 5:8), and that to receive eternal life he needed to receive Jesus Christ as his Savior (Romans 10:9–10). I then asked him if he would be willing to receive Jesus Christ as his Savior and nothing happened. He would not squeeze my hand either "yes" or "no." I repeated the question and received the same response—nothing. I repeated it once more with still no response. Then I waited for quite a long time and asked him one more time. But then, a strange thing happened. His wife spoke up and said, "For Pete's sake, squeeze the man's hand!" This jolted everyone in the room, but it got the desired response; I felt the squeeze for "yes" and proceeded with the prayer for his salvation. I asked him to repeat the prayer after me and asked him to respond if he had prayed the prayer. Happily, I felt the one-squeeze response, which told me he had received Christ. He died a short time later.

⊰ ANOTHER DYING FATHER ⊱

A frantic plea for prayer was received by one of our church ladies about her father. He was rushed to the hospital with an aneurysm in the main artery of his stomach. Another few minutes getting him to the hospital would have been fatal, according to the attending physician. But even then, he said, the situation was still very bleak after the surgery to repair the artery wall. He was placed in intensive care under the watchful eyes of specially trained nurses, who cared for him around the clock. When I arrived at the hospital and saw him with all the IVs and tubes throughout his entire body, I felt all I could do was pray for him because he was in a semicomatose condition. He did survive and eventually was moved to a private room. It was there I was able to make his acquaintance. We talked at some length about his daughter. I told him what a faithful church member she was, helping out at various functions and volunteering for many needed services. He told me how she had always been the apple of his eye. This was the best way for me to establish some kind of relationship. My further visits exposed his love for the game of golf and the fact that he had been the starter at one of the local golf courses. I told him I had played there and that he was probably the starter, but neither of us had known the other at the time.

It was amazing, but he improved quickly and was moved to an institution for his rehabilitation. It was there that I began visiting him weekly. Before long, we had a meaningful relationship established to the point that I felt it was time to start witnessing to him. His daughter told me that he had no religious background and, to her knowledge, had never attended any church. Because of this, I began my witness slowly, dropping bits of wisdom very carefully. For example, I mentioned that the doctors could do surgery and bind his wounds, but only the Lord could heal him. He agreed, and I told him of the numerous occasions I had seen the Lord do great things for people who trusted in Him. I would also spread Bible stories throughout our conversations when the subject matter allowed it.

Finally, after quite a few weeks, I felt it was time to really get serious about witnessing to him, and it was amazing how easily the door was opened to do this. It was a bright and sunny summer day when I entered his room and found him in a particularly good mood. We exchanged greetings and began our usual small talk when I became very serious and said that I thought it was time to talk honestly about eternal life. I said I would like to tell him of a very religious man who did not have the foggiest idea about how to get to heaven until Jesus told him. I asked him if he were interested in hearing the story, and he seemed excited to listen. I then told him the story of Nicodemus. He listened intently as I mentioned how Nicodemus was a leader of the Jews who recognized Jesus as a teacher from God and a doer of miracles; apparently Nicodemus had come to Jesus to ask Him about heaven, but never got the chance to ask. Jesus knew why Nicodemus had come; He said to him, "Except a man be born again, he cannot see the kingdom of heaven" (John 3:3). This blew Nicodemus's mind, and he completely misunderstood that Jesus was speaking spiritually about being born again, because he asked, "How can a man be born when he is old? Can he enter the second time into his mother's womb, and be born?" (John 3:4). Jesus patiently explained that being born of the flesh is one thing, but being born of the Spirit is quite another (John 3:6). Being born of the Spirit is like the wind blowing: you know it is there, but you cannot see it (John 3:8). In other words, Jesus was saying: just as no one enters this physical life without being born into it, neither can one enter heaven without being born into it. The physical birth is our entrance into our earthly family, just as the spiritual birth is our entrance into our spiritual family.

That Nicodemus was still confused became evident by his next question: "How can these things be?" (John 3:9). This question brought a completely unexpected response from Jesus: "Art thou a master of Israel, and knowest not these things?" (v. 10). That is, "Why, in all your many studies, have you not been taught the most elementary spiritual matters?" Yet, again, the Lord gives another earthly illustration to prove to Nicodemus that he needed something more than book knowledge to find the real truth. He had already given him the earthly illustrations of the birth experience and the wind; Jesus then gave him a story from the Old Testament to show him his need. The story is recorded in Numbers 21:6–9, where we are told that God sent poisonous snakes to bite the people for their continual griping about not having bread and water and not being satisfied with the manna given them. As a result of having been bitten, the people finally admitted they had sinned and asked Moses for a remedy to their predicament. The Lord told Moses to erect a pole with a brass snake on it in the wilderness. God promised that when anyone who had been bitten would come to the pole, he would live. Then Jesus compared Himself to that symbol saying He would be lifted up (on a cross) and all who come to Him would live forever (John 3:14–15).

After relating this story, I asked my friend if he were willing to come to the Savior and receive Him as his Lord, and he said he was willing. We prayed and I could imagine there was rejoicing in heaven over this one sinner who repented. There certainly was rejoicing in that hospital room that day and later, when his daughter learned that her dad was now a Christian. He met his Savior in heaven only a few short weeks after meeting him that day in his hospital room.

⊰ A DYING BROTHER ⊱

A member of my church asked me to pray for her seriously ill brother but stopped short of asking me to visit him in the hospital. I asked for the name of the hospital, which she reluctantly gave me with a warning. She was unsure of the reception I would receive if I called on him. He was a devout follower of another religion and had no sympathy for any but his own. I assured her I would be all right and scheduled a visit that week. I entered his room with my brightest smile and introduced myself as his sister's pastor. I explained that she was concerned about him and wondered if I would go by and pray for him. He accepted me, and we began to exchange information about each other. He told me of his medical condition, and I told him of my background as a hillbilly from Tennessee who got transported to Michigan to introduce some Southern culture to these rather uncultured

Yankees. This gentle kidding drew a smile, and the ice was broken. We spent several more minutes talking about current events, and then I asked his permission to pray for him and left. The initial contact in a difficult situation like this is all-important. It is imperative to establish a comfortable, nonthreatening atmosphere to set up the absolutely necessary visits in the future. The only spiritual thing I did was pray, and no one who suspects they may die will object to that.

I made many weekly visits after that and finally came to the point that I could introduce some Scripture verses into our conversation. One day, I quoted a verse that appropriately fit our conversation, and he said, "I wish I could do that." I did not understand what he meant and asked, "Do what?" He replied, "Be able to quote the Bible to fit each topic of conversation." I said, "You can, but you would have to study to get good at it." Then I added, "Here, I will leave my Bible with you so you can get started with your study. You have a lot of time on your hands right now, so this would be a good time to begin." He took the Bible, and I had prayer and left. When I returned the next week, I asked him if he had begun his study, and he said he had been reading, but he did not understand it all. I told him I would explain the things he did not understand and began giving him salvation verses such as John 3:16, 5:24; 1 John 5:11–13. He listened well, but I did not press him for a decision at that time. I felt he needed time to allow this scriptural truth to sink in. Eventually, he improved to the point he could go home, and I asked if I could continue to visit him at home and he consented.

At home the situation was much improved because there were no nurses coming in every few minutes to interrupt our conversation. When I arrived at his home each time, his wife would let me in and then disappear to another room, leaving us to have our private conversations. Finally, the day arrived that I felt I must approach him about giving his soul to Jesus. He greeted me in his usual friendly way, and we caught up on world events for the first few minutes. Then the inevitable lull in the conversation happened. I took this opportunity to pose a question to him. I asked, "_____, have you been thinking about where you would go if you were to die? You, know, I have shown you in the Bible many verses about eternal life, and you know that someday you will die. You do want to know that you would go to heaven, don't you?" He said he did, and I then asked him if I could show him from the Bible how he could know, and he replied in the affirmative. I then proceeded to explain salvation through the Romans Road: that he was a sinner (Romans 3:23); that because of his sin he must die (5:12); that Jesus died for his sin (5:8); and that he must receive Jesus as his Savior to be saved (9:10–13). Then I asked if he would like to receive Jesus right then, and he said he would. We prayed, and he asked Jesus to be his Savior. I will never forget the look on his face afterward. The lights really came on for him. His whole attitude changed, and his transformation proved once again that religion is powerless to do what only Jesus can do. Religion can reform, but only Jesus can transform. Religion can dress one up, but only Jesus can dress one with the heavenly white robe of salvation. Religion can make one respectable, but only Jesus can make one holy. Religion can give one temporary satisfaction, but only Jesus can give one permanent peace. Religion may make one happy, but only Jesus can give one real joy. And religion may give one a sense of security, but only Jesus can give one the rock-hard security of the promise, "Because I live, ye shall live also" (John 14:19).

Chapter 18

My Struggle to Help Others Struggle to Freedom

"*W*here's it say that in the Bible?" asked the new lady in my wife's weekly ladies' Bible study class. The questioner was a lady who had been brought to the class for the first time by one of the members. But it was not just once that she asked the same question. One could tell she was hearing things for the first time and, in her ignorance born of hearing Bible truth for the first time, wanted to be sure the teacher was not just making things up.

Carole and her Al were very devout. He taught confirmation classes at their church, and she tended to the local pastor as if he were a member of her family. Nearly every morning, she would go to his house and prepare his coffee and spend time talking over the happenings of the day. But when she began attending the ladies' Bible study, she began asking him questions like, "How come you never taught us we had to be born again to go to heaven?" He had no answer to her questions, but he did catch on to what she had been doing and asked, "You have been attending a fundamentalist Bible study, haven't you?" She answered in the affirmative but persisted in her questioning as to why he had not been teaching the truths she was learning from the Bible. The fact that he could not answer her brought great sadness to her heart, and she prayed that he would come into this knowledge until the day he died several years later.

She was not unlike many today who are very conscientiousness about their religion, but who are totally ignorant of what the Bible teaches about salvation. There are myriads of people in all religions who are in the same state. I happened to be a member of a Protestant church many years before I learned the way of salvation. Paul the apostle was a confirmed Jewish leader, but did not understand true salvation until his experience on the road to Damascus (Acts 9:1–20). This lady was like many people who believe that because they belong to a church that automatically makes them a Christian. But Jesus told a religious man, a leader in his church, that being religious is not enough; He told him he had to be born again to go to heaven (John 3:3, 7). Peter added some time later that the born-again experience takes place by virtue of the Word of God. That is, the Word of God is the instrument that imparts the knowledge that one needs to be saved before he can go to heaven.

We learn that Jesus was born to "save his people from their sins" (Matthew 1:21); that He came "to seek and to save that which was lost" (Luke 19:10); and to save, not destroy (Luke 9:56) (which explains why He did not resist being crucified). Salvation is not found in a church, a creed, or a manner of living; it is found in receiving Jesus Christ as one's Savior. Jesus challenged the religious leaders of His day to "search the scriptures; for in them ye think ye have eternal life: and they are they which testify of me. And ye will not come to me, that ye might have life" (John 5:39–40). Even though they were religious leaders, they were under the false assumption that because they had studied the Scriptures, they had eternal life. In reality, because they would not come to Him, they were lost.

This same couple's story began when the husband attended a class at a local university and one of the professors ripped into the book of Romans in the Bible with such ferocity that the husband surmised that, if the professor hated it that much, he should read it for himself to find out why he hated it so. To the man's great surprise, he found the great truths of salvation there and became so excited that he told his wife she should read it because of the wonderful truths it contains. Well, she was not all that hip about reading and gave mental assent, but she knew she would never do it. About this same time, a neighbor invited her to attend the ladies' Bible study at our church, and she, seeing a way to study the Bible without too much effort, accepted her neighbor's invitation. It was at this first meeting that Carole asked all the questions, but the truths being taught piqued her interest and kept her coming back. It was not long until the couple began attending our church, even though things had not gelled in either of their minds. Soon, we received a phone call inviting my wife and me to come to their home and answer some questions. On the first visit, we stayed until nearly midnight, answering their questions with Bible passages. Their main concern was whether they would have to leave their church if they accepted the teachings of the Bible. They really loved their church, and they expressed how beautiful the services were and how much they loved their pastor. I told them it was not my place to tell them what to do and that they could go to their heavenly Father and He would give them their answers. The husband had come to the Lord by reading the book of Romans and his wife received the Lord at the end of one of the ladies' Bible study classes. We were at their home many times after this, answering their questions late into the night. Each time, we noticed how much they both were growing in the Lord.

He eventually became one of the deacons in our church and she became very active in food preparation. She became a very bold witness for the Lord and still takes every opportunity to tell people about her wonderful Lord. He taught computer science at a local college for many years and let his faith be known in his classes. Both are jewels in Christian faith and are continuing on in faithfulness to their Lord. Both their daughters graduated from a Christian university and both married fine Christian husbands.

⇒ε GOD'S TIMING ⇒ε

Another couple moved toward freedom in Christ through a unique instance of God's timing. Ordinarily, our church secretary left the office at 5:00 P.M., but one day she was detained by extra work and by waiting for her husband to pick her up. The phone rang at 7:00 P.M., and the woman's voice on the other end wanted to speak with the pastor (yours truly). The secretary explained that I had gone for the day, but wondered if she could help. The lady insisted that she must speak with the pastor, so the secretary suggested they set up a time when I could visit them in the home, and they agreed upon a time.

At the appointed time, I appeared at their home. They were a young couple, probably in their early thirties at the time, with four children. One more would be born to them a few years later. They lived in a small, three-bedroom brick home in a lower-middle-class neighborhood. They had the appearance of what one would consider the makings of an ideal situation, but there was soul trouble in this home. They had been attending a church but were dissatisfied with its social emphasis over its spiritual emphasis. They knew there was something better but did not know how to find it. The lady told me she had opened up the phone book and had begun calling churches. She had determined that whichever one answered would be considered to be the one they would attend. I asked her what she would have done if our secretary had not answered that day, and she said she would have kept trying until one answered. This confirmed to me that our church was God's choice for them.

I began by asking about their salvation experiences. She spoke up and said she had been saved as a child but had grown cold in her spiritual growth. Further questioning revealed she did not have any assurance of her salvation. When my attention turned to her husband, I noticed he became quite squeamish and at first tried to avoid my question about whether he had ever been saved. Finally, he admitted he had never been saved, and I asked if I could show him how to know he was saved. I began showing him the Romans Road. When I came to the point of asking him whether he would be willing to accept Jesus as his Savior, he balked. He was not sure it would work with him, he said. I found out later that he was a very moral person and proud of his morality. I was told he lived a much better life as an unsaved person than many saved people. But I could see he was gripped by the convicting power of the Holy Spirit, and I proceeded to try and convince him to give his heart to the Lord right then.

Nothing seemed to work until I gave him an illustration to show him all he needed to do was to make the initial movement toward the Lord, and He would be there to receive him. I described a little child, like his daughter, on a high platform, with her father down below urging her to jump and assuring her he would be there to catch her. At that moment, he jumped up from his chair, excused himself, and hurried out of the room. He later told me he left the room to weep and was ashamed to weep before me. I also learned later that he dearly loved his daughter, and the illustration had struck a nerve. When he reentered the room, I asked him again if he would accept Christ, and he agreed. He prayed one of the most heart-wrenching prayers I had ever heard and was promptly ushered into the family of God with the angels in heaven rejoicing again that a sinner had repented.

The whole family began attending our church, and, in time, all four children were saved and the entire family was baptized on the same night. Both father and mother grew quickly in the knowledge of the Lord and before long took on responsibilities in the church and Sunday school. He was an avid outdoorsman and would take the boys from his Sunday school class on overnight camping trips. He treated those boys like his own and took them other places as well. He became a deacon and contributed greatly to the leadership of the ministry. He made sure that when his one daughter and four sons grew up, they would attend a Christian university. All five of them attended a Christian university and three of the five are in full-time Christian work at this time. The timing of the Lord was certainly at work when the secretary was detained long enough to receive that all-important phone call.

My struggle to freedom has been long and sometimes arduous, but the freedom attained has been worth every minute of it. The peace I have attained has been indescribable and wonderful. No more do I have to worry about what other people think, I just have to be concerned about what the Lord thinks and He is much easier to please than people. What a wonderful Lord!

Chapter 19

MY STRUGGLE WITH PURITY

My wife asked once whether I could ever be unfaithful to her after learning a pastor friend had committed adultery. My answer startled her. I told her I could, but by God's grace and her prayers I would be able to remain faithful to her as long as I lived. I could not dogmatically say that I would never fall into sin, but my desire and intent was that I never would. I am so determined to remain faithful that I prayed before we married that if I ever became unfaithful the Lord would kill me on the spot. Needless to say, that prayer keeps me on guard because I believe God would take me at my word. There are other ways I safeguard myself. I counseled a lady one time whose husband left her for a younger woman. In the course of a conversation we had she said she wished her husband had the characteristics I had. I could see where this was going so I headed her off by stating, "I am what I am because of my wife." The shock on her face proved she got my point.

When I have a wrong thought I expose it immediately to the Lord's light. When the back of a camera is opened it exposes the film to the light and washes it out. The Lord's light is much more powerful than a camera's lens and He has never failed to wash away my wrong thoughts. Dire consequences come to those who choose adultery. Not only is there terrible guilt, but there is an embarrassment in facing members of one's own family. The guilty party thinks he will never be found out, but the scripture promises "Be sure your sin will find you out" (Numbers 32:23). Scripture also promises other consequences. "So is he he who sleeps with another man's wife; no one who touches her will go unpunished" (Proverbs 6:29 NIV). "But a man who commits adultery lacks judgment; whoever does so destroys himself" (Proverbs 6:32 NIV). "Blows (wounds) and disgrace are his lot, and his shame will never be wiped away" (Proverbs 6:33 NIV). Some guilty pastors cannot live with the shame and have taken their own lives. Adultery is a horrifying experience.

The tendency for a man is to look first at a lady's figure. Bill Gothard gives good advice in his seminars by advising men to look only at her face and never at her figure. Sensual looking seems to be the gateway to wrong thoughts, which sometimes leads to other forbidden activities. Eve looked first at the fruit then acted on what Satan said (Genesis 3:5-6). We are told in Proverbs 5:18 to "rejoice with the wife of thy youth" and verse 19 says to "be thou ravished always with her love." The word "ravished" can also be translated "intoxicated." In other words, "be thou intoxicated with her love." I have made it a practice to confess to my wife any wrong thoughts I may have about other women and she is very gracious and forgives me. My reluctance to perform this embarrassing confession helps me keep my thoughts pure, but even then there are times I fail and am forced to go through the ritual again.

✄ MARRIAGE IS A SACRED RELATIONSHIP ✄

My relationship to my wife is a sacred union. The Lord

compares it to His relationship with the church (Ephesians 5:30,32). Every marriage is backed by the sovereignty of God. The man who says, "I don't love her anymore" is either focusing on her faults or he has designs on another woman. Love is not something you take off and on like a coat. The sovereignty of God cements that marriage together and to break it apart flaunts the will of God. Since love is not a feeling, but an act of the will, he is actually saying, "I am not willing to love her anymore." He uses all the ammunition he can muster to make his reason for not loving her more respectable. He could claim he was forced to marry her because he made her pregnant or he gave in to public pressure and her persistent insistence to marry her. But the fact remains that God does not change His sovereign will about marriage, regardless of the man's flimsy excuses. Not loving one's spouse is never given as a cause for divorce in scripture. The solution is to will to love her. God will give strength to anyone who makes the effort to love his mate. In your courting days it was no effort to love her. Forget her faults and look at her as she was then. Remember your own faults and work on them and you will be so busy you will not have time to see her faults.

⊰ THE PREVALENCE OF INFIDELITY ⊱

Infidelity tempts almost every man whether an unbeliever or believer. One of the most spiritual men in the Bible, David, succumbed to it. It is a sin that stalks men especially, but pastors seem especially susceptible. The Detroit News, February 29,1988, reported 300 pastors were asked if they had an sexually inappropriate relationship with someone other than their spouse. Twenty-three percent said they had. Twelve percent said they had intercourse with a person other than their spouse, eighteen percent admitted to other forms of sexual contact with another person. The other party came from a variety of positions, such as the person being counseled, a staff member, a staff member from another church, a church member in a teaching-leadership role, a member of the congregation or someone outside the congregation. Many and varied are the stories of ministers who have slipped into immorality.

⊰ Husbands are to Love Their Wives ⊱

It is clear that husbands are to love their wives as their own bodies (Ephesians 5:28). This is difficult because men are by nature egotists. In almost every desperate situation men will look out for themselves first. During the yellow fever epidemic in Memphis, TN, 1873, mothers stayed with an infected child even if they contracted the disease, but not the husbands. They deserted their families and quickly ran to safe places. The husband who helps with the housework or looks after the children is a rarity. The formula is simple: just love your wife to the same degree you love yourself. That he loves himself is a no-brainer. God says, "He who loves his wife loves himself" (Ephesians 5:28). There is no separating husband from wife because they are "glued" together (Genesis 2:24). "Cleave" means to be glued together.

⊰ Satan's Persuasive Powers ⊱

The temptation to stray is so subtle that one almost feels justified in his infidelity. Satan's persuasive powers he uses on men is not unlike what he used on Jesus. He tried to persuade Jesus turning stones into bread was a legitimate need (Matthew 4:3-4). He tries to persuade men that involvement with another woman is a legitimate need, and that his wife no longer meets that need. He may grow tired of her and thinks another woman will somehow meet that legitimate need. But the only legitimate need of husbands is to love their wives.

Satan also uses man's penchant to be admired or praised to cause him to stray. The other woman provides the admiration he loves, which causes him to fantasize about her beauty (Proverbs 6:25). Proverbs warns about the immoral woman and her "smooth tongue" (6:24), "her seductive words" (7:5), and her "smooth talk" (7:21). Satan tried to use this tactic on Jesus by persuading Him to jump form the highest point of the temple and let the angels catch Him (Matthew 4:5-7), which would bring admiration and praise from the people. The Lord rebuked him by stating one should not allow himself to be put in a position that forces God to act (Matthew 4:7). The husband who becomes involved in an illicit affair forces the intervention of God, which brings misery and heartbreak and severe judgment. If he had done what the Bible says, "For if we would judge ourselves, we should not be judged" (1Corinthians 11:31). Self-judgment eliminates God-judgment.

✂ Satan's Inferior Offers ✂

Satan's inferior offers are always inferior to God's superior blessings that come from waiting. Jesus turned down the immediate offer of bread to the superior blessing of angels attending Him (Matthew 4:11). Dr. Bob Jones Sr. used to say we were never to sacrifice the permanent on the altar of the immediate. To have an affair is to sacrifice honesty, loyalty and reputation on the altar of immediate desire. The thief gives up character on the altar of immediate greed. I returned to my car one night after attending a ballgame to find a thief had broken in and stolen my tape player. I was furious until I realized the thief had paid for his action by his loss of character. He paid for his greed with his character. The murderer gives up peace on the altar of anger, jealousy or hatred. Giving in to immediate desire loses much more than it gains. Satan's offers are proffered with convenience. It is always more convenient to sin than to wait for God. Satan made it convenient for Jesus to sin just as he makes it for us. But Jesus chose to wait for God's blessings. I waited for the wife of God's choice and fifty-nine years of marriage proves it was right to wait.

Conclusion

As you make your struggles to freedom, you may be thinking they are too hard and you may begin to have thoughts of giving up. I know, I was there. Many times I thought, "it just isn"t worth the time and effort to keep on plugging away to an uncertain end." I felt like the psalmist in Psalm 73, who named all the good things that were happening to the wicked and all the bad things that were happening to him, the so-called righteous one. This was not supposed to be happening to a believer in the Lord. He felt that way until he changed his focus from himself to God. When he finally did that, he could say of the wicked, "Surely Thou dost set them in slippery places; Thou dost cast them down to destruction" (Psalms 73:18 NASB). And later, he said, "But as for me, the nearness of God is my good; I have made the Lord God my refuge, that I may tell of all Thy works" (v. 28 NASB).

I found new strength of purpose when I made God my focus. He gave me something to live for - to please Him. It was no longer what would please me, but what would please God. I found that when I sought to please Him, I lost sight of what would please me. It didn't matter anymore that the struggles were too hard because now I could see a purposeful end. Pleasing God had its fulfillment in giving me a sense of purpose, knowing I had done the right thing. Great satisfaction comes from knowing one has done something good.

My friend, as you have read the pages of this book, my prayer is that you have sensed the presence of God in every word and that the author would not even enter the picture.

Appendix

(The following is primarily for the pastors who might buy the book. Anyone else who wants to read it might find it interesting).

Funerals

I shall never forget the first funeral I preached at the first church I pastored. Shortly after I arrived, I was asked to preach the funeral of a man I had visited just once. I had never preached a funeral and had attended very few in my lifetime. "What was I going to do?" I wondered. My liberal arts curriculum did not include Funerals 101. Funerals were a lot more complicated then than they are today. Fortunately, the family asked another pastor to assist me; he was to read the Scripture and I was to do the preaching, but it turned out he was to do a lot more than reading the Scripture. I said to him, "Look, this is my first time of conducting a funeral. Could you guide me through since you are a veteran pastor?" He did, and I made it through just fine.

Over the years, I learned there is much more to conducting funerals than just preaching a message. At a funeral seminar I attended, I learned that the purpose of funerals was for the family to work out their grief. A funeral was not to be an evangelistic service, but an opportunity to minister. People are grief stricken and need to hear words of comfort. This does not mean I do not present the gospel, but I present it gently, "speaking the truth in love" (Ephesians 4:15), rather than calling fire down from heaven.

People do get offended by a wrong attitude displayed by the pastor. I have discovered if I preface my remarks with a simple disclaimer, as it were, it disarms any negative response they may have. I say, "I have a threefold responsibility. First, I am a minister of God called to preach God's Word in truth. Second, I have an obligation to relate to you what I think the deceased would say if he/she could speak. And third, I feel a tremendous obligation to present the truth about life and death in as simple and understandable a language as I can manage." That takes care of the sourpuss looks I get. They think I'm just doing my job. I never put anyone in heaven unless I am sure they went there, and I never put anyone in hell, either. I just preach what is necessary to go to heaven.

It is a good idea to have someone in the family present a eulogy, especially if I did not know the deceased. It takes the pressure off me to say something about the deceased. I think it is dishonest to make something up about the individual no matter how general it may be. "He was a good man." How do you know he was a good man? He may have been the meanest man in the county. You may use something a family member told you about him at the viewing, but please don't make something up just to have something to say. If you feel you must say something about the individual, get with the family on the night of visitation and quote them.

Eulogies saved my neck one time. I was asked to conduct the funeral of a person I had never known and there was no visitation the night before, so I could get no information from family members. This was cold turkey; I felt I should say something to soften the harshness of the Bible. A Bible message is offensive enough by itself, but even more so if not predicated by at least a few descriptive words about the character of the deceased. Time came for me to preach. I stood before the crowd, wondering what to do when, in a flash, the Holy Spirit gave me the solution. I asked if anyone had anything to say about the deceased. To my utter amazement, six people rose to their feet and gave glowing testimonies of character of the deceased. I was saved! And I was able to go on and preach the gospel with the assurance that people listened because nice things were said about the deceased.

Sermon Outline

At just about every funeral I preach, I use this outline.

WHAT DEATH IS TO THE CHRISTIAN IT IS "GOD WITH US" (Matthew 1:23)

John Wesley's final words: "The best of all, God is with us."

"Yea, though I walk through the valley of the shadow of death, I will fear no evil: for thou art with me" (Psalm 23:4).

Stephen, the first martyr: "Behold, I see the heavens opened, and the Son of Man standing on the right hand of God" (Acts 7:56).

"Lo, I am with you alway, even unto the end of the world" (Matthew 28:20).

IT IS THE END OF FEAR, WORRY, SICKNESS, SORROW, AND FAILURE

Fear becomes peace.

Song sung by Christians at the catacombs: "Good night, beloved, sleep and take your rest, Lay down your head upon the Savior's breast."

Worry becomes trust.

Sickness and sorrow are removed forever: "And God shall wipe away all tears from their eyes" (Revelation 21:4).

Failure becomes victory.

"But thanks be to God which giveth us the victory through our Lord Jesus Christ" (1 Corinthians 15:57).

IT IS THE FULFILLMENT OF THE PROMISE OF ETERNAL LIFE THROUGH JESUS CHRIST

He has abolished the penalty of death: "Jesus Christ… hath abolished death, and hath brought life and immortality to light through the gospel" (2 Timothy 1:10).

He has given power over death: "If a man keep my saying, he shall never see death" (John 8:51).

He has removed the fear of death.

I FEAR NOT DEATH

I fear not death, I long to die,
And in the narrow grave to lie
Disturbed not in my quiet rest,
My spirit with the saved and blest.
The coffined bed, the shroud, the bier,
Possess for me no shade of fear;
How quickly would I welcome all,
And calmly smile beneath the pall.
Earth has no charms to bid me stay
Within this body's worthless clay:
But Heaven has charms so great and fair
I long to rest in safety there.
Teach me, dear Lord, to be content,
And that my life be fitly spent;
I wait with patience for the day
When Christ shall bear my soul away.[18]

He has removed the sting of death: "O death, where is thy sting? O grave, where is thy victory?" (1 Corinthians 15:55).

My hourly glass is nearly run,
My days and deeds will quickly pass;
And yet my life has just begun
For death will but invert the glass.[19]

He has given a different meaning to death: "Christ has made of death a narrow, starlit strip between the companionship of today and the reunion of tomorrow."[20]

Dying words of the saved:

Edwin Abbott: "Glory to God! I see heaven sweetly opened before me!"

Dwight Moody: "This is glorious! Earth receding, heaven opening. God calling me!"

John Antler: "The chariot has come, and I am ready to step in."

John Lyth: "Can this be death? Why, it is better than living! Tell them I die happy in Jesus!"

Margaret Pryor: "Eternity rolls before me like a sea of glory!"

Mary Frances: "Oh, that I could tell you what joy I possess! The Lord doth shine with such power upon my soul. He is come! He is come!"

Mel Trotter: "I am in perfect peace, resting alone on the blood of Christ. I find this amply sufficient with which to enter the presence of God."

DEATH OF THE CHRISTIAN IS PRECIOUS IN THE LORD'S SIGHT

"Precious in the sight of the LORD is the death of his saints" (Psalm 116:15).

DEATH OF THE CHRISTIAN IS GAIN

Men have vainly tried to soften the harshness of the word death:

Walt Whitman: "Cool-enfolding death."

Robert Ingersol: "The fine serenity of death."

William Shakespeare: "A necessary end."

Paul gives the Christian view: "To die is gain" (Philippians 1:21).

There is eternal bliss: "In thy presence is fullness of joy; at thy right hand, there are pleasures for evermore" (Psalm 16:11).

There is eternal companionship.

Words of an aged Scotsman: "If I die I will be with Jesus; if I live, Jesus will be with me."

No man ever repented of being a Christian on his death bed.

DEATH OF A CHRISTIAN IS HIS TIME FOR US

"The LORD gave, and the LORD has taken away, blessed be the name of the LORD" (Job 1:21).

Illustration—Two words on the tombstone—"Freddie!" (his name is being called to come to heaven), "Yes" (he is answering the call in the affirmative).

Weddings

Next to funerals I hate to conduct weddings the most. They are too formal and ceremonial to suit me. I like for things to be relaxed and informal. I get a kick out of the flower girl tripping over the top step and falling down with her dress coming up over her head And then there is the ring bearer. I remember once during a ceremony, I saw something out of the corner of my eye, something that appeared, and then disappeared, appeared, then disappeared. When I turned to get a better view, I saw the ring bearer tossing the pillow in the air and catching it. He was just having fun and could care less about anything else that was going on. I envied that little kid.

There is much more to weddings than the ceremony. The ceremony is the culmination of many hours of premarital counseling that went on before. I made it a rule that I would not marry anyone until they had submitted to at least eight weeks of counseling. I use a program published by Life Innovations, Inc., Prepare/Enrich, Box 190, Minneapolis, MN 55440–0190. The web address is *www.prepare-enrich.com* and the phone number is 1–800–331–1661. You need to know how compatible the couple is, and this program gives you that knowledge.

The problem for the pastor is how to convince the church girls not to marry these bums they drag into his office. Before I started using this program, I just flew by the seat of my pants (mainly the Holy Spirit). On one occasion, I refused to marry a couple because I was not convinced he was a Christian. He became furious, stomped out of my office, went up the street, and found a pastor who would marry them. Not a month later he was picked up by the police for propositioning an undercover officer from the police department.

Another occasion brought what I thought was a wonderful Christian couple to be married. I used the program and found they were woefully incompatible. They made the worst score I had ever seen. I advised they not get married, but they were sure they could overcome their weaknesses, and I married them against my better judgment. Theirs was a stormy marriage, to say the least. After they settled into their marriage, problems arose, and they came to me for counseling. They each had a list of complaints against the other. I noticed their lists of praise for the other were missing. As I counseled them, I noticed they had set boundaries that told the other to stay out of their territory; if they crossed over, they would be severely punished. Marriage is to be a sharing experience, not a punishment. A sharing of joy and pleasure and, if need be, of pain. They work on their problems together, not separately.

I saw this solution pictured with two donkeys tied together, each struggling to eat their bales of hay just out of reach. The next picture showed them with a question mark over their heads, as if to say, "Why are we struggling to reach our hay separately when we would have no problem working together?" The final pictures showed them working together and eating their hay—first the one bale, then the other. I told the couple they could accomplish much if they would just work together. They were acting like five-year-olds demanding their rights.

In marriage there are no rights, only privileges. I do not have the "right" to be happy, if I do not earn that right by making sacrifices. Marriage offers us privileges when we make sacrifices. When we make the sacrifice of quality time spent with each other, we enjoy the privilege of being adored by our mates. By quality time I mean doing something I really don't enjoy because I know my spouse likes it—like shopping. I personally would rather have a root canal than go shopping, but I will go shopping because I know my spouse likes it. True happiness comes from denying yourself to make someone else happy. We are to give in order to receive (Luke 6:38). The couple was not willing to make the necessary sacrifices and was divorced a short time later.

Baptism

I do not believe in immersion because I am a Baptist, but I do believe immersion is the scriptural mode of baptism. At the baptism of Jesus, the Scripture says, "Straitway coming up out of the water, he saw the heavens opened" (Mark 1:10). I believe it is a picture of the death, burial, and resurrection of our Lord. I also believe it is a picture of our identification with Him in His death, burial, and resurrection. Having said that, I do not believe one has to be immersed to go to heaven because baptism is a work and we are not saved by works. Dr. Bob Jones, Sr. used to say a person can go to heaven if he is dry-cleaned. As long as a person has received Jesus Christ as his Savior and is trusting Him and the work He did for us in taking away our sins, I believe he will go to heaven whether he is immersed or sprinkled.

Nither do I believe one will go to heaven BECAUSE he has been baptized, whether by sprinkling or by immersion. Many people believe their baptism is their salvation. I have asked a number of people on what basis do they believe they would go to heaven. They reply, "Well, I was baptized on such and such a date." Oh no, that is not the correct answer. Salvation is in a Person. "Neither is there salvation in any other: for there is none other name under heaven [Jesus] given among men, whereby we must be saved" (Acts 4:12). "He that hath the Son hath life; and he that hath not the Son of God hath not life" (1 John 5:12). "He that believeth on the Son hath everlasting life: and he that believeth not the

Son shall not see life; but the wrath of God abideth on him" (John 3:36).

Notes

Chapter 7

1.   William B. Gamble, Benedicte's Scrapbook (Grand Rapids: Eerdmans, 1954), 129.

Chapter 8

2.   Walter B. Knight, Knight's Master Book of New Illustrations (Grand Rapids: Eerdmans, 1956), 231–232.

Chapter 9

3.   Jay Adams, The Chrisitan Counselor's Manual (Grand Rapids: Zondervan, 1973), 378.
4.   Ibid.

Chapter 10

5.   Walter B. Knight, Knight's Master Book of New Illustrations (Grand Rapids: Eerdmans,), 1956, 207.
6.   Kenneth S. Wuest, Word Studies in the Greek New Testament, Vol. I (Grand Rapids: Eerdmans, 1961), 221.

Chapter 11

7.   Dennis Guernsey, Sometimes It's Hard to Love God (Downers Grove, IL, InterVarsity, 1989), 11.

Chapter 12

8.   W. E. Vine, An Expository Dictionary of New Testament Words, Vol. 3, 1940, 18, No copyright
9.   Marvin R. Vincent, Word Studies in the New Testament, Vol. III, 1887, New York, New York

Chapter 14

10.	Walter B. Knight, Knight's Treasury of Illustrations (Grand Rapids: Eerdmans, 1963), 244.

11.	Eleanor L. Doan, The Speakers Sourcebook (Grand Rapids: Zondervan, 1960), 18.

12.	Walter B. Knight, Knight's Master Book of New Illustrations (Grand Rapids: Eerdmans, 1956), 446–447.

13.	Walter B. Knight, 3000 Illustrations for Christian Service (Grand Rapids: Eerdmans, 1963), 245.

14.	Walter B. Knight, Knight's Master Book of New Illustrations (Grand Rapids: Eerdmans, 1956), 449–450.

15.	Walter B. Knight, Knight's Treasury of Illustrations (Grand Rapids: Eerdmans, 1963), 245.

16.	Roy B. Zuck and Gene A. Getz, eds., Adult Education in the Church (Chicago: Moody, 1970), 101–102.

Chapter 15

17.	Kenneth S. Wuest, Word Studies in the Greek New Testament, Vol. II (Grand Rapids: Eerdmans, 1978), 64.

Appendix

18.	William B. Gamble, Benedicte's Scrapbook (Grand Rapids: Eerdmans, 1954), 76.

19.	Ibid., 76

20.	Ibid., 77